Following His Footsteps (I):
"Lessons from the Life of Jesus"

© By Dr. Randall D. Smith

These volumes were prepared with students and teachers of the Bible in mind. The series is taken from the actual teaching notes of Dr. Smith as he teaches through all of the Bible each year at Great Commission Bible Institute in Sebring, Florida.

Table of Contents

Following His Footsteps:
Lesson One: "Jesus is for Losers" (Matthew 1, Luke 3)

Today I want to introduce the most important figure in my life. I first heard of Him as a child, but didn't meet Him until I was in High School. He continues to be my friend, counselor and constant companion through each of the seasons of my life... but He is much more than even those words can describe. He is also my Master, my Sovereign, my King and my Lord. He has no equal – not in my life, and not in the cosmos. There truly is NONE like Him, and there is no real and lasting answer found in any other. I want you to meet Jesus, not just in this lesson, but in a whole series of what the Bible records about Him. I want to look at His life, not in bits, but rather as one story – one harmonized story of the Savior. That is what this new series of lessons is all about. That means, we will leave our normal "book study" method, and be looking at four presentations of Jesus – side by side – the four accounts we call the "Gospels". In fact, I want to take you to three passages in this lesson – each expressing the beginnings Gospel accounts, and begin to unpack the story of Jesus.

Before I do, I have to admit something. I believe wholeheartedly that Jesus is for LOSERS. A careful study of what He said and did will reveal, I believe, that He did not come for the strong, but for the weak. He did not come for the self-satisfied, but for the bankrupt in spirit – struggling souls who know that they have shipwrecked their lives by their own choices. Those who feel they can navigate life without Him will choose to do so. Some will call them "arrogant", but the Bible calls them simply "fools". I am no fool, but I am a loser. I am not a loser because of what I was when I found Jesus – but rather because of what Jesus told me to DO as a result of knowing Him. I was called to LOSE... but more about that a bit later....

Jesus came to change us. He was an example – but that wasn't His primary goal. He was a helper to the fallen and weakened, the social outcast and the religious flunkie – but that wasn't His main purpose. Jesus came to wipe out the atonement system –

the "kill a goat for God" and replace that whole system with permanent, complete and total justification. He came to set us free from sin – the Bible repeats the claim again and again. In His redemptive plan, He also came to challenge us to surrender to God our lives as He surrendered His for us. He came to move us from where we were when we met Him, to where He intended us to be – in His service. The opening verses of the Gospel accounts will help us see a truth very clearly…

Key Principle: Christianity isn't merely a belief system, it is a movement. It requires more than mental assent to a list of facts; it requires deliberate opening of my heart to God's transformation of my life.

The Gospel writers were very open about what they wanted to present. They offered a clear picture of Jesus, and desired to enlist a clear response. Here is the truth: the Biblical notion of faith requires surrender or it is neither faith nor Biblical. That is a fact historic believers recognized that seems to be obscured in our time. Let's look at how the writers shared Jesus.

First, the record of Jesus was presented with a <u>clear purpose</u>:

*Luke: 1:1 Inasmuch as many have undertaken to compile an account of the things accomplished among us, 2 just as they were handed down to us by those who from the beginning were eyewitnesses and servants of the word, 3 it seemed fitting for me as well, having **investigated everything carefully** from the beginning, to write [it] out for you in consecutive order, most excellent Theophilus; 4 **so that you may know the exact truth about the things you have been taught**.*

Our faith is built on a **set of truths** that were **passed** to us, and must be **accepted** (Luke 1:1-2a). Let it be clear to all who embrace the Bible and its message that our faith is defined by the text, and recorded by our earlier faith family.

Our faith came from **eyewitness testimony** that followed Jesus from the beginning of the story, not **loose rumors and idle imaginings** from centuries after the fact (Luke 1:2b). The Bible is clear, and a simple sample makes the demand clear:

*2 Peter 1:16 says "For we did not follow cleverly devised tales when we made known to you the power and coming of our Lord Jesus Christ, but we were **eyewitnesses** of His majesty...21 "for no prophecy was ever made by an act of human will, but men moved by the Holy Spirit spoke from God."*

*2 Tim. 3:16 "All Scripture is **inspired** by God and profitable for teaching, for reproof, for correction, for training in righteousness"*

Luke reminds us that our faith is rooted in an **actual story** that had both a progression of events, and evidence that these events were **real** (Luke 1:3). He was able to interview people, collect accounts, and gain evidences. He did his homework with a surrendered heart and the Spirit's leading – and we have the product of his work.

Sir William Ramsay (15 March 1851 – 20 April 1939) was a Scottish scholar that undertook careful archaeological research to test the authenticity of the account of the Gospel of St. Luke. He began his work as a skeptic of the Bible, and was educated at the Universities of Aberdeen, Oxford and Gottingen, Exeter College, Oxford, and Lincoln College. In 1885 he was elevated to the position of Professor of Classical Art at Oxford, and in the next year Distinguished Professor of The Humanities at Aberdeen. He was immersed in the skeptical teaching that prevailed in his day, but forced himself to search for primary source materials and evidences that would lead him to a conclusion very unlike his peers of the day. After careful research, Ramsay astounded his fellows with the belief that the Gospel of Luke was actually written by Dr. Luke, and that it shared historically accurate information. After a time, Ramsay further concluded that the evidence he saw led him to believe the message of the Gospel of Luke – that Jesus WAS, in fact, the Messiah and Lord. He began his career as a mocker and skeptic, but closed his career as an ardent defender of the Gospel accounts.

Luke also made the point that our faith must be **grasped from the text** of the Scriptures, for they possess the **exact truth** about Who and what Jesus is (Luke 1:4). This isn't a "I feel Jesus is this way" kind of faith. Our feelings are subject to the text – because it offers the true view of the Person of Jesus.

It is also worth noting that Luke made clear that our faith leads us to **certainty about God and His work in us.** Modern "scholarly mysticism" has made uncertainty into a "Zen-like" positivism – as if KNOWING makes one at least weak and at worst bigoted. It seems in the modern classroom, the only person considered a true scholar is the one who claims that "little or nothing can be truly known". The Biblical message stands opposed to that sentiment. Note that Luke wrote that "**you many know**" (1:4) to a group of Jesus' early followers. The purpose of the Gospels was not to offer a string of myths and pithy sayings that may or may not have come from the mouth of Jesus of Nazareth. The purpose of the Gospel record was to document the account and accurately record the history of a real man that walked on the earth, in order that believers would be able to fully grasp the model and meaning of Jesus' life and work.

In times of trouble, fluffy feelings of camp Christianity won't hold us together. In persecution, general musings about Jesus just simply won't do. In times of searing pain, the weightless Hallmark Jesus won't get us through the tears of the night. God offered SUBSTANCE in the "four windows into the life and work of Jesus" because He knew well that **we would need carefully examined structures and principles that will help us when the world refuses the truth** and the winds of culture turn coldly in the face of the Christian!

Jesus was truly introduced by the Gospel recorders with A CLEAR PURPOSE in their accounts, but that isn't all...

The record of Jesus was also presented with some <u>clear implications</u>:

The record of Jesus MEANS SOMETHING. It isn't simply the introduction to an ancient mythical hero like Achilles or Ulysses. This record is meant to CHANGE THOSE WHO ENGAGE IT. It forces us to look not only at the FACT of His coming, but the implications of that coming to the way that we conduct our lives. Take a few minutes to consider the ways Jesus was exposed in the narrative, and the implications will become quite clear.

First, Jesus came in the flesh, not as a simple mythical action figure of campfire stories. He is not "man idealized" as German skeptical scholars tried to cast. He came as a child into a real family, birthed from a real womb and suckled by a real woman. This tale was one of cold nights, uncomfortable journeys, near death traps, and nosy shepherds. It was the tale of a real child born into a real cave stable and warmly wrapped in cloth and placed in a pile of hay.

While we introduce Jesus in the records, we have to admit that there are TWO GENEALOGIES of Jesus presented by the evangelists – one in Matthew's opening verses, and one in Luke 3:23 ff. Side by side, they offer some interesting and important opening notes about the record of the Savior that we don't want to skip. Don't flinch when you read the two accounts – Matthew and Luke – and find that they don't agree. Remember, if the account were "doctored" by the church, every place the accounts didn't match they would have been "edited" to do so. The fact that two genealogies are left in the text speaks to the veracity of the accounts. At the same time it begs the question: "Is one of them faulty?" Obviously, as one who believes in the historical veracity of the text, I would say a firm "No!" Yet, some explanation is necessary.

Look at Luke 3, and you will read a litany of unfamiliar names – all are offered to carefully demonstrate **Jesus came as an Israelite child:**

Luke 3:23b "....being, as was supposed, the son of Joseph, the son of Eli, 24 the son of Matthat, the son of Levi, the son of Melchi, the son of Jannai, the son of Joseph, 25 the son of Mattathias, the son of Amos, the son of Nahum, the son of Hesli, the son of Naggai, 26 the son of Maath, the son of Mattathias, the son of Semein, the son of Josech, the son of Joda, 27 the son of Joanan, the son of Rhesa, the son of Zerubbabel, the son of Shealtiel, the son of Neri, 28 the son of Melchi, the son of Addi, the son of Cosam, the son of Elmadam, the son of Er, 29 the son of Joshua, the son of Eliezer, the son of Jorim, the son of Matthat, the son of Levi, 30 the son of Simeon, the son of Judah, the son of Joseph, the son of Jonam, the son of Eliakim, 31 the son of Melea, the son of Menna, the son of Mattatha, the son of Nathan, the son of David, 32 the son of Jesse, the son of Obed, the son of Boaz, the son of Salmon, the son of Nahshon, 33 the son of Amminadab, the son of Admin, the son of Ram, the son of Hezron, the son of Perez, the son of Judah, 34the son of Jacob, the son of Isaac, the son of Abraham, the son of Terah, the son of Nahor, 35 the son of Serug, the son of Reu, the son of Peleg, the son of Heber, the son of Shelah, 36 the son of Cainan, the son of Arphaxad, the son of Shem, the son of Noah, the son of Lamech, 37 the son of Methuselah, the son of Enoch, the son of Jared, the son of Mahalaleel, the son of Cainan, 38 the son of Enosh, the son of Seth, the son of Adam, the son of God.

His lineage is presented in **reverse order of history**, moving backward from Jesus' parent to Adam, summarizing generations. Three important observations are in order:

First, "**son**" in antiquity was used for "descendant" and could mean a direct son, or a grandson of any generation following the father. Therefore, Luke included forty-two names in the list, while Matthew only included twenty-six names – each are legitimate records of "son ship". The fact that Matthew omits names can be cross checked in the passages in Kings and Chronicles easily.

Second, Luke makes the point that the **genealogy is "unusual" in that Jesus' legal father was not His actual father**. Note the awkward wording of Luke 3:23 "being, as was *supposed*, the son of Joseph". Clearly the genealogy, were it to be that of Joseph, had a "legal character", but **did not represent the "physical genealogy" of Jesus** – for He will be clearly presented by the same author as "from the Holy Spirit" and not from the "seed from a man". This led many church historians to believe (as I do) that this genealogy is that of Mary's line, leading to her grandfather Eli. Early church historians recognized this possibility, though some of them (like Julius Africanus in about 240 CE) that perhaps both were of Joseph's line - and Eli was Joseph's legal father while Jacob was his physical father. Before we get lost in the detail of that view, let's just simply say it this way… If Joseph's mom married Eli, but he died without leaving an heir, Eli's brother Jacob could have fathered a child in the place of his brother (what was called a Levirate marriage) to raise up the name of the dead brother Eli). It is nice to know that families were NEVER simple! Some early church historians thought this was the case, but I am not convinced.

Third, the simpler understanding may be that **Luke presented the PHYSICAL line of Jesus through the line of Mary, while Matthew presented the LEGAL line of Jesus through Joseph** – His LEGAL dad. The reasons for this view are carefully documented in Thomas and Gundry's Harmony of the Gospel (pp. 316-317), and need not be dissected in this summary.

The bottom line of the two accounts is this: **Jesus was a Jewish little boy, a son of the tribe of Judah, born through the womb of a young woman**. Though conceived through a miraculous act of the Spirit, His birth was conventional and physical. This fact will be explained again and again in places like Hebrews and Galatians – because it is necessary to understand the story.

In Matthew's account, the baby was not simply a Jewish child – but **Jesus came as an heir to the Judah's throne:**

*Matthew 1:1 The record of the genealogy of Jesus the Messiah, the son of David, the son of Abraham: 2 Abraham was the father of Isaac, Isaac the father of Jacob, and Jacob the father of Judah and his brothers. 3 Judah was the father of Perez and Zerah by Tamar, Perez was the father of Hezron, and Hezron the father of Ram. 4 Ram was the father of Amminadab, Amminadab the father of Nahshon, and Nahshon the father of Salmon. 5 Salmon was the father of Boaz by Rahab, Boaz was the father of Obed by Ruth, and Obed the father of Jesse. 6 Jesse was the father of David the king. **David** was the father of Solomon by Bathsheba who had been the wife of Uriah. 7 **Solomon** was the father of Rehoboam, **Rehoboam** the father of **Abijah**, and Abijah the father of **Asa**. 8 Asa was the father of **Jehoshaphat**, Jehoshaphat the father of Joram, and **Joram** the father of **Uzziah**. 9 Uzziah was the father of **Jotham**, Jotham the father of **Ahaz**, and Ahaz the father of **Hezekiah**. 10 Hezekiah was the father of **Manasseh**, Manasseh the father of **Amon**, and Amon the father of **Josiah**. 11 Josiah became the father of **Jeconiah** and his brothers, at the time of the deportation to Babylon. 12 After the deportation to Babylon: Jeconiah became the father of Shealtiel, and Shealtiel the father of Zerubbabel. 13 Zerubbabel was the father of Abihud, Abihud the father of Eliakim, and Eliakim the father of Azor. 14 Azor was the father of Zadok, Zadok the father of Achim, and Achim the father of Eliud. 15 Eliud was the father of Eleazar, Eleazar the father of Matthan, and Matthan the father of Jacob. 16 Jacob was the father of Joseph the husband of Mary, by whom Jesus was born, who is called the Messiah. 17 So all the generations from Abraham to David are **fourteen** generations; from David to the deportation to Babylon, **fourteen** generations; and from the deportation to Babylon to the Messiah, **fourteen** generations.*

At least **fifteen names off the Matthew's list** are easily identifiable as **ancient kings of Judah**. In the midst of the account, the claim was made three times that an even span of "fourteen generations" existed between Abraham and David,

David and Babylon, and Babylon to Jesus – a claim that a modern student may find difficult because it is simply not true to the account of the Hebrew Scriptures. The issue was the indicative devise from first century numerology, common to the ancients, but lost in modernity.

In the ancient near east, much was made of the juxtaposition of names with their "numerical equivalents". In Revelation 13:18 the "Antichrist" had a name that was numerologically determined as "666". In Matthew, the name DAVID is the number fourteen – and the issue Matthew was driving at was that Jesus was of DAVIDIC ROYAL DESCENT. Matthew consciously chose the numerology and it was significant to early believers in Jesus, but the devise has been lost in modern generations.

Here is the point: Jesus came as KING. His was the position of RIGHTFUL SOVEREIGN – not a simple and humble teacher from the Galilee hills. He was a promised ruler, and will one day show exactly what that position means – but you must stay tuned for the Second Coming of Messiah.

Jesus came as an Israelite priest:

When we cited Luke 3, we skipped the first few words... Yet, in them is another piece of the story line... Note in Luke 3:23 the words: "When He began His ministry, Jesus Himself was about thirty years of age..."

Jesus began a "ministry" or "priestly work" when He was the age of inauguration of service for that purpose – age thirty (2:23). If He began His work at the time of a priest, could it be that His work was intended to be seen as priestly? Of course it can...

The point of all this information is this: Jesus was real child, born to a real mother, in a real village. He came as a promised king, and did the work of a Temple priest. All these truths have implications for how we respond to Him.

If He is a King – I am not his equal.
If I am His subject – than His desires and direction for my life are more significant that my own.

If He came as man – than God literally poured Himself into the form of human flesh for my salvation – a fact that should stop me in my tracks. The God of Wonder, the Master of Heaven cares about my lost state, and wants me to know Him!

If He came as a priest – I have One that can take me by the hand and lead me into God's presence and full acceptance.

It is true there was a clear purpose in the story of Jesus, and that His positions have clear implications for us, but that is not all...The record of Jesus offers a clear portrait:

Look at the rich words of John's introduction to Jesus. The text alternates between words about John and about Jesus. I am selecting out the verses dedicated to the introduction of the Savior in 1:1-5; 1:10-18

John 1:1 In the beginning was the Word, and the Word was with God, and the Word was God. 2 He was in the beginning with God. 3 All things came into being through Him, and apart from Him nothing came into being that has come into being. 4 In Him was life, and the life was the Light of men. 5 The Light shines in the darkness, and the darkness did not comprehend it...10 He was in the world, and the world was made through Him, and the world did not know Him. 11 He came to His own, and those who were His own did not receive Him. 12 But as many as received Him, to them He gave the right to become children of God, [even] to those who believe in His name, 13 who were born, not of blood nor of the will of the flesh nor of the will of man, but of God. 14 And the Word became flesh, and dwelt among us, and we saw His glory, glory as of the only begotten from the Father, full of grace and truth. 15 John testified about Him and cried out, saying, "This was He of whom I said, He who comes after me has a higher rank than I, for He existed before me.'" 16 For of His fullness we have all received, and grace upon grace. 17 For the Law was given through Moses; grace and truth were realized through Jesus Christ. 18 No one has seen God at any time; the only begotten God who is in the bosom of the Father, He has explained [Him].

Look carefully at the portrait of Jesus, because John knew Him very well. John followed Jesus, sat in warm rooms and listened to the Master's teaching for hours on end. He stood horrified at the Cross, watching his mentor breathe His last breath. He was qualified to offer a close-up view of Jesus... Here is what he carefully shared:

First, John said that Jesus already **existed before the creation** of the physical world with His Father – the Creator God. He was the Word (1:1,15) for He was the One that came "and dwelt with us" (in 1:14).

Second, John claimed that His Savior was the very **CREATOR of all that existed** (1:2-3). John was not unaware of Genesis 1, but rather agreed with Paul's words to the Colossians 1:16:

"For by Him all things were created, [both] in the heavens and on earth, visible and invisible, whether thrones or dominions or rulers or authorities-- all things have been created through Him and for Him. 17 He is before all things, and in Him all things hold together."

John even added that ABSOLUTELY NOTHING exists that He didn't create (1:3).

Third, John made the case that Jesus **brought the light of truth to a deceived mankind**, and that light **burned** their eyes.

Max Lucado tells the story about a tribe of people who lived in a dark, cold cave. The cave dwellers would huddle together and cry against the chill. Loud and long they wailed. It was all they did. It was all they knew to do. The sounds in the cave were mournful, but the people didn't know it, for they had never known joy. The spirit in the cave was death, but the people didn't know it, for they had never known life. But one day they heard a different voice. "I have heard your cries," it announced. "I have felt your chill and seen your darkness. I have come to help you." The cave people grew quiet. They had never heard this voice.

Hope sounded strange to their ears. "How can we know you have come to help?" "Trust me," he answered. "I have what you need." The cave people peered through the darkness at the figure of the stranger. He was stacking something, then stooping and stacking more. "What are you doing?" one cried, nervously. The stranger didn't answer. "What are you making?" another shouted even louder. There was still no response. "Tell us!" demanded a third. The visitor stood and spoke in the direction of the voices. "I have what you need." With that he turned to the pile at his feet and lit it. Wood ignited, flames erupted, and light filled the cavern. The people turned away in fear. "Put it out!" they cried. "It hurts to see it." "Light always hurts before it helps," he answered. "Step closer. The pain will soon pass." "Not I," declared a voice. "Nor I," agreed a second. "Only a fool would risk exposing his eyes to such light," said another. The stranger stood next to the fire. "Would you prefer the darkness? Would you prefer the cold? Don't consult your fears. Take a step of faith." For a long time no one spoke. The people hovered in groups covering their eyes. The fire builder stood next to the fire. "It's warm here," he invited. "He's right," one from behind him announced. "It is warmer." The stranger turned to see a figure slowly stepping toward the fire. "I can open my eyes now," she proclaimed. "I can see." "Come closer," invited the fire builder. She did. She stepped into the ring of light. "It's so warm!" She extended her hands and sighed as her chill began to pass. "Come everyone! Feel the warmth," she invited. "Silence woman!" cried one of the cave dwellers. "Dare you lead us into your folly? Leave us. Leave us and take your light with you." She turned to the stranger. "Why won't they come?" "They choose the chill, for though it's cold, it's what they know. They'd rather be cold than to change." "And live in the dark?" she asked. "And live in the dark," he replied.

Now we return to our opening… we who are called to Jesus are called to be LOSERS. We LOSE our own vision, and grab the hand of the Master of light. We lose self-determination of our life's course, and we allow Jesus to take the lead. We do it because He is our KING. We do it because He is our CREATOR. We do it because HE UNDERSTANDS what life here is all about. We do it because the record concerning Him is the TRUTH!

Lessons from the life of Jesus (1)

The world persists with the claim that we follow "cleverly devised myths". Jesus was a **fake** and there is **no God**. When we die, there is **nothing** else. God is a creation of the human **mind**. A hapless **accident** caused the world you see, the heavens in their expanse. Planets spin and whirl according to no particular design. The delicate web of cells that make the flowers of the field such a wondrous beauty are a cosmic fluke. There is <u>no</u> <u>plan</u>. There is <u>no</u> **future**. Man is an **animal** among the evolved DNA strands of the universe… **yet you should behave and try to find meaning**. You should do things to benefit others. You should care about how poor and suffering people live. You should try to keep the planet green. We should advance the knowledge of the species. **We should live well and seek a meaningful life where – we essentially agree - there is none. Why?**

The unbeliever offers a sad picture, but without a personal experience with God it is not hard to understand. One cannot see God by looking at **RELIGION**. In fact, religion more illustrates man's hard heart and ego filled soul than the goodness of God. In the name of religion wars rage across the planet. One cannot see God by looking at **MORALITY** and **CONSCIENCE** for these change with the tide of public opinion in the age. No, to really understand God, you must **MEET** Him and have His eyes pierce your heart.

There is an old saying: ""If at first you don't succeed, find out if the loser gets anything as a consolation prize." I am here to tell you the LOSER WINS.

I titled this message "Jesus is for Losers" and I meant just that. We who follow Jesus are called to "**lose our life**" to Him. We are called to recognize that this **Jesus was shared with a clear purpose**, with clear implications concerning His holy work. We possess a clear portrait – but none of that makes any difference unless it transforms who we are. Mental assent acknowledging the existence of God won't change my destiny – deliberate surrender of my life choices to Jesus will. Why? Because…

Christianity isn't merely a belief system, it is a movement. It requires more than mental assent to a list of facts; it requires deliberate opening of my heart to God's transformation of my life.

Following His Footsteps:
Lesson Two: "Changed by the Pain" (Luke 1:5-80)

Pain changes you. I was speaking the other day to a friend who has been caring for his wife through a recent cancer surgery. He was encouraged at her progress, and she is doing well. As he spoke, he reminded me that this was her third cancer surgery – and that she had learned some important things that she passed to her husband. She called cancer "the great clarifier". When the treatments were a memory and the pain had mostly passed – she was able to see her life more clearly than she ever could before. It was the trouble of her life, the threat to its continuance here on earth that gave her a different perspective. She was changed by the pain. She was transformed by the threat, the discouragement, the questions toward God and the world – and she emerged a different woman.

I am glad that I had that simple encounter the other day, because her simple lesson encouraged me to think about life in deeper terms. In the business of the daily, the broader picture of things can be obscured. Thank God He places people in our lives to cause us to pick up our heads from the task before us, and think about the distant horizon and where we are going.

As I work with believers of all ages, I think I begin to recognize some of the wisdom of God in placing us together in the local body of believers. Some among us have passed through enormous pain – the loss of a dream, the loss of the love of our lives, the loss of our health and physical stability. Sitting beside them at any given meeting are others who believe deeply, but have experienced little. They are not to be belittled, for their zeal and their energy are essential to the progress of God's church – but they really don't have that much experience, thankfully, with deep pain and disappointment.

Tucked between the two groups are "game changers". These are people that have both experienced the pain, and kept the optimism and belief. They are the un-jaded sufferers among us that help all of us keep things together. They know what it is like to be discouraged – they have visited that address, but they have refused to move in and live there. They have felt the searing pain that comes with living in a fallen world, but they have found God's balm of healing, and have moved on. They are the heroes and heroines of our story – and they have found a voice in Luke's recorded story of Elizabeth. Here is the lesson…

Key Principle: Younger and older believers need each other. Some of the most learned believers are in the process of growing past their troubles while some of the most uninitiated can profoundly speak – but they haven't been tempered by the troubles ahead. God uses the one who has been changed by the pain to teach both to move ahead with Him.

For the Bible students among us, I would like to take a moment and see if I can make clear how I came to the conclusion that this was the key truth at the heart of Luke 1. If you read through the entire chapter, you will notice if falls into three "natural" parts:

- The story opened with the angel Gabriel foretelling of a son to a Senior Priest named Zecharias at the Temple. He was accomplished in ministry, but operating with a whole in his heart when it came to vibrant faith. (Luke 1:5-25). In a sense, Zecharias was jaded by the long trail of troubles unanswered in his life and he silently returned home to the encouragement of his loving wife at the end of the segment of the chapter given to his announcement.

- Luke recorded yet another story of a similar announcement - a message of an exciting coming birth. The angelic announcer was the same. The conditions were the same – she was working on her daily tasks with no thought of anticipation. The key difference was the attitude and experience of the hearer. (Luke 1:26-39) Mary was tender of heart, but also very young and lacking the experiences of pain. Her scene ended with a trip to the very same encouraging woman Zecharias went home to live with.

- Both scenes have their representative song – an anthem about God and His fulfillment of promises. Mary's song flowed from her heart went Elizabeth encouraged her firm belief (Luke 1:46-46). Zecharias' song took longer, because it came from beneath scars of trouble, and didn't come until his faith was fully restored (Luke 1:57-80).

When you look at the whole of the chapter, you quickly note some similarities in two stories of the same chapter:

1. Two people who knew and served God were living their lives and doing their daily duties.
2. Both received an astounding visitor from Heaven that came to give them exciting news.
3. Both got a promise of an addition to their family.
4. Both were promised that the coming child would change the world.
5. Both got a prophetic song that was so important, it was included in the Scripture.
6. Both got their encouragement from the same lady (Elizabeth) – an experienced woman who both loved God, and knew pain.

At the same time, you cannot read this chapter and not notice some startling differences in the two people who encountered God's messenger…One went through **years of pain and doubt** before the message, and couldn't just accept it when it came; he demanded proof, and needed time to be encouraged to see things differently. The other spoke joyously of the promise, but didn't yet know **how difficult it was going to be to live through the pain** of that promise. She had no clue what the snickers at the well of town would feel like, or how hard it would be to tell her fiancé of the promise.

The most exciting person in the narrative wasn't the angel that encountered both people – it was Elizabeth. She encountered both of them, knew them both very well, and had passed through the pain in a way that would help both of them gain a proper footing to be used mightily by God. **God uses the one who has been changed by the pain to teach both.**

With that overview in mind, let's take a few minutes in this lesson and look at each of the three sections of the story, and see if we can recognize what Elizabeth took away from her pain that can help all of us:

Zacharias and the Problem of Jaded Faith (Luke 1:5-25)

You don't have to be walking in rebellion to have a faith "cooled" by the pain of disappointment. Look at the way Zach is introduced…

*Luke 1:5 In the days of Herod, king of Judea, there was a priest named Zacharias, of the division of Abijah; and he had a wife from the daughters of Aaron, and her name was Elizabeth. 6 They were both **righteous** in the sight of God, **walking blamelessly** in all the commandments and requirements of the Lord.*

How do I know they weren't perfectly happy then? Because the rest of the story makes clear that their home was filled with a hole – a pain that bothered both Zach and Liz…

*Luke 1:7 **But they had no child**, because Elizabeth was barren, and they were both **advanced** in years…24 After these days Elizabeth his wife became pregnant, and she kept herself in seclusion for five months, saying, 25 "This is the way the Lord has dealt with me in the days when He looked [with favor] upon [me], to take away my **disgrace** among men."*

The text reminds that Liz felt "disgrace" over being barren. The term "óneidos" means "defamed, reproached, censured, and even blamed". Don't you wonder what was behind that loaded word? In any case, "disgrace" is not a term you use for a happy feeling in an idyllic home. Liz was an embarrassed wife, and she was married to a disappointed husband. Her aging priestly husband prayed and prayed that God would give them a son – but God didn't answer the way Zach wanted Him to respond. Zach wanted a baby – and **so did God**… but God's plan was **much** bigger. It always is when God says "No!"

God never refuses to give you what you want because He is mean or doesn't love you. He only refuses to give you what you want if it is too small for His plan for you. God wanted a "miracle baby" that would profoundly change the people's hearts – beginning with the heart of his dad. Zach just wanted to feel normal. **His request was far too small for God's big plan.**

Enter **providence** – the word that has been replaced in a pagan culture by "**coincidence**"… God was about to put "points on the score board":

*Luke 1:8 Now it happened [that] while he was performing his priestly service before God in the [appointed] order of his division, 9 according to the custom of the priestly office, **he was chosen by lot to enter the temple of the Lord and burn incense**. 10 And the whole multitude of the people were in prayer outside at the hour of the incense offering. 11 And an angel of the Lord appeared to him, standing to the right of the altar of incense.*

The priestly job given to Zach was to represent the prayers of the people of God in the Temple. All Jerusalem awaited on the time of the incense to loft their prayers up to God. Ironically, the guy who felt the worst about prayer was given the task of representing the prayers of all. God not only noticed… He pre-planned the whole event to get Gabriel the angel into the room, and make clear what the next part of the plan would be for Zach and his wife… and the whole of the nation!

Gabriel related in Luke 1:12-17 that Zacharias' wife would have a baby, that it would be a boy, and that Zach was to name the child "Yochanon": (The Lord has been gracious). That baby was going to grow up, be used by God's Spirit, and challenge the whole nation of Israel. He would come in the place and power of

Elijah in announcing Messiah... This boy was going to be like a prophet of old....**How exciting!** Yet, the next words out of the mouth of the old priest showed like a clean window the jaded color of his heart... He asked for proof...

Luke 1:18 Zacharias said to the angel, "How will I know this [for certain]? For I am an old man and my wife is advanced in years."

Look carefully at what Zach said. Had they "thought" on a few occasions that Liz was pregnant, only to have that hope crushed? Besides, Zach was no fool. He knew his own age, and he knew his wife's potential for having a child had long left... He knew what we all know when God wants to do something incredible...."WE CAN'T!"

We can't make life from old bones. We can't fight physics, aging or science. We are stuck with what is... unless God wants to re-write the script. What we forget is that God is not bound to the rules of the world – He is the Ruler of it all!

Stunned, Gabriel didn't get it. He came from Heaven, and brought his message. What kind of being doesn't get that God can do whatever suits His plan? In two words, jaded believers. When you have asked and asked – and hurted with each rejection – you start to think God isn't looking out for you at all. In those dark hours, it never occurs to you that God is the one that put you where you are, because He has a plan at work.

Luke 1:19 The angel answered and said to him, "I am Gabriel, who stands in the presence of God, and I have been sent to speak to you and to bring you this good news. 20 "And behold, you shall be silent ... 23 When the days of his priestly service were ended, he went back home.

The believer who cannot believe God needs to keep his mouth shut. He isn't going to be obedient in proclamation, nor encouraging in delivery. He is going to whine and doubt – and that helps no one. God made it clear to everyone that He was at work – that God had spoken... and then God took Zach's voice for a time – to get the point across to HIM before God used him to get it to anyone else. Zach wanted proof – and he got it. He was mute. Everyday he couldn't speak he would recall that meeting with Gabriel wasn't an apparition – it was an event. Then his mind would recall the message of that meeting. God was about to do something…

What I find interesting is that he went home to an encouraging, believing wife. She KNEW God was going to remove her disgrace long before her belly swelled. She heard and believed, anticipated and celebrated. He was quiet because the jaded heart was being recolored by a miraculous God.

Mary and Naïve Faith

Move to the other main story of Luke 1 – that of the familiar meeting in Nazareth between Mary and Gabriel. The time for this lesson is tight, and the story familiar, so let us look at the high points to grab the main truth of this incredibly rich and cosmos changing event. The story can be broken into three parts:

- Gabriel's announcement to Mary (Luke 1:26-38);
- Mary's encouraging visit to Elizabeth (Luke 1:39-45);
- Mary's song of celebration called the "Magnificat" (Luke 1:46-56).

In the meeting story of Luke 1:26-38, we are dropped into the scene as Mary encounters the angelic messenger…

Luke 1:26 Now in the sixth month the angel Gabriel was sent from God to a city in Galilee called Nazareth, 27 to a virgin engaged to a man whose name was Joseph, of the descendants of David; and the virgin's name was Mary. 28 And coming in, he said to her, "Greetings, favored one! The Lord [is] with you."

Beyond the startled nature of the appearance, Gabriel explained that God was going to fill the womb of Mary with the One that was long promised. Messiah was to be born in her, as God had promised through prophetic voices of the Hebrew Scriptures...Look at Mary's response:

Luke 1:34 Mary said to the angel, "How can this be, since I am a virgin?" 35 The angel answered and said to her, "The Holy Spirit will come upon you, and the power of the Most High will overshadow you; and for that reason the holy Child shall be called the Son of God. 36 "And behold, even your relative Elizabeth has also conceived a son in her old age; and she who was called barren is now in her sixth month. 37 "For nothing will be impossible with God." 38 And Mary said, "Behold, the bondslave of the Lord; may it be done to me according to your word." And the angel departed from her.

Mary offered no doubt that God COULD do these things, only that she didn't understand the mechanics. Was she being told to DO something? Gabriel was clear – she needn't worry about the conception – God was handling that issue. She offered consent beautifully.

Now wait... this begins to sound like Zach was the old crusty and jaded priest, and Mary was the pure-minded, always obedient servant. That's fine. It fits the flannel graph and matches the history of church art. Mary the pure, Zach the deficient...but is that REALLY FAIR?

Is it fair to say that Mary had not lived with snickers at the well like Elizabeth did? Is it fair to say that Zach had much more experience in trying to be encouraging to a humiliated life partner than Mary ever could have understood? My point is this: Mary quickly embraced God's vision for her – but was far too naïve to really understand what pain she was buying into. Zach may have hesitated much more, but he had much more history behind him. Let's not be so hasty to paint perfectly adorned togas on the good guys in the Biblical story. The jaded had the pains that left the cloudy marks on their heart.

Stop for a moment, and go to the pivotal character of the whole story – the woman that suffered pains but clung to her faith...

Elizabeth and Firm Faith

Follow Mary to the meeting with Auntie Liz...

*Luke 1:39 Now at this time Mary arose and went in a hurry to the hill country, to a city of Judah, 40 and entered the house of Zacharias and greeted Elizabeth. 41 When Elizabeth heard Mary's greeting, the baby leaped in her womb; and Elizabeth was filled with the Holy Spirit. 42 And she cried out with a loud voice and said, "**Blessed [are] you** among women, and **blessed [is] the fruit** of your womb!*

Listen to the sound of encouraging words that came from her mouth. Elizabeth was EXPERIENCING God's interruption of grace in "real time", when Mary stepped through the door. Before the Magnificat was sung, the senior believer, scarred with years of disgrace, was singing the celebration of a GOOD GOD!

Freeze the scene and remember what Elizabeth went through to get to that place in her heart. Neighbor after neighbor celebrated their pregnancies with gifts from Elizabeth's hands – but there was never any such celebration in Zach and Liz's home. Morning after morning Liz made her way with the other women to get water from the nearby spring for their daily needs. All the while as the women walked they talked, "How little Eli is growing" and "What to do about Miriam's bed wetting". Liz kept silent, and held back tears because God evidently didn't think she needed... or worse... deserved children. The water she brought back in her pot was nothing compared to the tears that stained her face when she finally got back inside. Month after month she begged God for a baby, but with each month's passing, she felt both more helpless and more forgotten. Was Zacharias angry with her? Even if he didn't SEEM like it, did he hold HER to blame inside?

Look at the way she handled the news that God heard her prayer:

Luke 1:24 After these days Elizabeth his wife became pregnant, and she kept herself in seclusion for five *months, saying, 25 "This is the way the Lord has dealt with me in the days when He looked [with favor] upon [me], to take away my disgrace among men." Later, when Mary came, you hear her voice again...43 "And how has it [happened] to me, that **the mother of my Lord** would come to me? 44 "For behold, when the sound of your greeting reached my ears, the baby leaped in my womb for joy. 45 "And **blessed [is] she who believed** that there would be a fulfillment of what had been spoken to her by the Lord."*

Here is the Elizabeth picture sketched out:

- She knew pain, but still believed God was good, and would deal with her in grace.
- She knew the impossible was made possible when God decided to touch her body.
- She knew it wasn't coincidence, because she took seriously the Word of God and the prophetic promises God made.
- She encouraged belief in Mary.
- She trusted that God was good, and that her rescue was because of His goodness.
- She refused to let the pain determine her view of God.

Let me ask you something..."Who are you in the story of Luke 1?" Are you working for God but **deeply jaded because He isn't doing things the way you want them** to play out in your life? Are you **anticipating great thi**ngs, and just "don't get" why some of those who have known God for a long time aren't more enthusiastic and excited about what the Master is doing right now? Could it be that **you may even be the one who has been tempered by God in trouble**, and right now God is nudging you to get busy helping those around you see God's faithfulness in spite of troubles.

Not everyone knows how to face pain and trouble – but God made some of us to help others figure it out...

One day a farmer's donkey fell down into a well. The animal cried piteously for hours as the farmer tried to figure out what to do. Finally he decided the animal was old and the well needed to be covered up anyway; it just wasn't worth the effort to retrieve the donkey. He invited all his neighbors to come over and help him. They all grabbed a shovel and began to shovel dirt into the well. At first, the donkey seemed to realize what was happening and cried horribly. Then to everyone's amazement, the beast quieted down. A few shovel loads later the farmer finally looked down the well and was astonished at what he saw. With every shovel of dirt that hit his back, the donkey was doing something amazing! He would shake it off and take a step up. As the farmer's neighbors continued to shovel dirt on top of the animal, he would shake it off and take a step up. Pretty soon, everyone was amazed as the donkey stepped up over the edge of the well and trotted off....There are a number of ways we can handle pain and trouble. It is easy to get discouraged and give up, or get angry and blow up, but if we really believe that God is in control, then we will look for a way to build our trust in Him to help us get through it His way.

Recognizing the True Hero

It is worth remembering that God's deepest work can be done by the one who has the scar-riddled body, when that one refuses to allow scars to be torn open and become scabs. The hero among us isn't the polished angelic messenger, nor the weathered and experienced believer – but the Faithful God each of the others represent before a lost world. God has a purpose for every pain in the story He is telling – and we must trust Him through each hurt. He also has a place for the wounded – as comforted testimonies for those who come behind them. **God uses the one who has been changed by the pain – provided that change has led the wounded into His arms.** The story of the Bible isn't about people who "figured life out" and "did the right thing". The story of the Bible is about a God who wouldn't leave broken people in the dark – and how He grabbed and holds them tightly.

Following His Footsteps:
Lesson Three: "Dad's Big Dreams" (Matthew 1 and 2)

One day a year we honor the place and work of fathers, yet all year long many of us have learned to appreciate the work they are called to do. I am a father, and now a grandfather – and I have been reflecting in the early morning hours during the feeding of "McGoo" (my nickname for my grandson Malachi) on the work God called men to do. It was fortuitous that the next page in our study of the"Life and Ministry of Jesus" as told by the four evangelists was about the stand-in man God chose to play the father's role in the life of Jesus as he was born in Bethlehem, fled to Egypt and later raised in Nazareth. It didn't escape my notice that not much was said about Joe.... It was my experience with my own dad that fathering was sometimes like that.

You see, my dad wasn't the "center stage" guy – but rather the quiet guy that dropped me off to the meeting and picked me up after it was over. He paid for my doctor and dentist visits, made sure they had purchased the necessary number of gym shorts for class, and took care of a tuition payment in a private, Christian school that could have easily made the payments for a new car every year. He did not stand on any stage, anywhere, and take a bow for what he did. He just did it, day in and day out...whether it was convenient or not, whether he felt like it or not. He never believed the modern myth that one can "have it all" – be a parent and still live for self.

In fact, it wasn't until my graduation from high school that I learned how dad provided for more than a dozen kids. I applied to join the labor pool of the oil refinery my dad worked at his whole career... and I discovered a place that was filled with vulgarity, pornography and cynicism. It wasn't that I didn't meet some really good guys there – it was the fact that I was, perhaps for the first time, exposed overtly to the world my father worked to provide me with something different – something better – something where God would be honored and not maligned daily.

In many ways, my father was a quiet disciple and provider that no one ever would be. My point is that like my dad, Joe didn't get a big stage and rousing applause from the crowd. He got the job of listening to God's direction and then leading based on what God revealed – which the real job of any man. Joe is listed in the earliest pages of the Gospels, and then, like many fathers, he fades to the background as the son or daughter pushes ahead, not recalling until later the platform from which they launched.

In some ways Joe's job was like any father – they were given a child by God, and they were to provide, protect and prepare them for the world they would face. Every dad has dreams for their child! In the case of sons in a godly home, they want them to be men of God, bold about their witness and loving and caring in their deportment. I cannot imagine that Joe's heart was any different... God chose the right man for the tough job ahead!

It's true that in SOME ways Joe's job was similar to other men... but in other ways, Joe's job was unique – beginning with the first public act a dad had in his time... **naming their son**. Joe didn't choose the name - God revealed what it was to be. From the time of the first revelation of God to Joe through a dream... Joe knew the truth: his job wasn't to live out his dreams through his son – but he would be a "stand in" for his Father in Heaven.

In this lesson, I want to share a story about **four** dreams. The first one was in the **heart of Joe before he ever knew Mary at all**. Joe wanted to be **significant**, and he wanted to leave a **legacy** that mattered – like every man who ever held their son in their arms. His **next four dreams** required that he **surrender his first dream to the Lord**, so that God could do MORE with his life than he could have ever understood at the time – and answer his deepest longings through a Son that would change the world forever! The key principle for Matthew's story of the beginning of Jesus' earth walk is derived from watching Joe:

Key Principle: God will lead you if you surrender to *His* story and not make your life about *your* story! (Mt. 1:18-25).

To delve into the Joseph story, we have to look into the beginning of Matthew's Gospel. Both Matthew and Luke record genealogies, but that isn't the only feature of the beginning stories of the "pre-ministry" they disclose...in fact, the two Gospel writers offered **details on several events** before explaining the launch of Jesus' earth ministry at His baptism by John in the Jordan River.

- Matthew focused on **how God directed Joseph**.
- Luke focused more on **right responses to the wondrous message that God sent Messiah**.

These are our next two lessons...one on Joe, and one on responses to God's gift of Jesus...Traveling through the Holy Land, year after year, I have often wondered what Joseph and Mary would say if, as they reflected back to the birth of Jesus, they sat and listened to our Christmas carols and watched our Christmas plays. Do you really think Mary thought it was a "Silent night, Holy night?" I don't know, but having been in the delivery room with each of my children...I am thinking she was just relieved the child was born and healthy... and she was probably exhausted.

Revealing Dream Number One:

Look at Matthew's account of what Joe went through, and let's see if we can pick out what he learned from the text...

Mt. 1:18 "Now the birth of Jesus Christ was as follows: when His mother Mary had been betrothed to Joseph, before they came together she was found to be with child by the Holy Spirit. 19 And Joseph her husband, being a righteous man and not wanting to disgrace her, planned to send her away secretly. 20 But when he had considered this, behold, an angel of the Lord appeared to him in a dream, saying, "Joseph, son of David, do not be afraid to take Mary as your wife; for the Child who has been conceived in her is of the Holy Spirit. 21 "She will bear a Son; and you shall call His name Jesus, for He will save His people from their sins." 22 Now all this took place to fulfill what was spoken by the Lord through the prophet: 23 "BEHOLD, THE VIRGIN SHALL BE WITH CHILD AND SHALL BEAR A SON, AND THEY SHALL CALL HIS NAME IMMANUEL," which translated means, "GOD WITH US." 24 And Joseph awoke from his sleep and did as the angel of the Lord commanded him, and took Mary as his wife, 25 but kept her a virgin until she gave birth to a Son; and he called His name Jesus."

Before drawing conclusions, look at the *details* of the text of Matthew 1:18-25:

First, the story was given to tell you the CONTEXT of the birth of Jesus (1:18a). Second, the TIMING of the pregnancy was clear – Joe had not "been with" her, and was unaware at first of who the father of the baby could be (1:18b).Third, the TROUBLES of Joseph show he was contending with many decisions (1:19-20a).

- He was a "righteous man", which may be a translation of the Hebrew idea of "tsaddik" – an elder in a congregation. If that was the case, the reputational troubles were not his alone, but would be shared by his congregation.

- He was a "tender man", and though he no doubt felt disrespected by her, he didn't want her to be subject to public derision.

- The angel's word to him in 1:20 shows that he was also a "fearful man" – unsure of what kind of woman Mary truly was, and how much he could even trust his own feelings and measures of what he thought she was. Whenever we are betrayed, some part of us blames ourselves for not perceiving more accurately the people that drew us into deception.

Now step back and look at REVEALING DREAM NUMBER ONE:

Mary was cleared of any guilt or wrong against Joe – the "guilty party" was God Himself (1:20). God's plan was made clear – a Boy was coming to save His people (1:21). This fit what God had already revealed in His Word (1:22-23). Joe was thoroughly convinced the dream was from God, and he did exactly what the messenger told him to do – despite what ANYONE in his life could have counseled him to do (1:24-25).

Joe might offer the lesson learned this way: "God works in ways I never would have imagined. One day you are just moving through life, living within the boundaries, and following God's Word, and the next thing you know... there is a whole new set of issues in your life! Here's the thing I took away from those early days... do what God says even when the outcome isn't clear. If it squares with His Word, it is truth no matter what all my friends think. If I obey what He has told me, He will direct my next steps into His will!"

In just a few verses, God offered a great thumbnail sketch of a man used by God in a powerful way! He lived inside the boundaries of sexual purity and obedience. He learned the Scriptures and led a community with a careful, circumspect life. He sheltered the reputation of people in the story, and he was pliable when God spoke into his life. His path changed when God ordered it to change and verified that word by Scripture. In the end, Joe was a good man because he was a willing follower of God's direction!

Can you see in Joe a faithful leader without a vindictive spirit when hurt. Can you imagine his initial confusion, his embarrassment – maybe even anger? Can you identify that although he lived within the law, he understood authority but still wanted to show mercy. Joe was no Pharisee – just a guy trying to follow God and not wound people in the process.

Here is the important lesson that we cannot miss in his life: Joe's fervent walk with God did NOT protect him from misunderstanding God's program. He responded to what God had revealed to him, and needed more revelation to alter course. Joe was told to abandon his plans to send her away –

an overt call to surrender control of the situation based on experience and trust God's Word. Joe was called to stop leading and FOLLOW. *Remember: some men won't take directions even when they are lost!*

Joe was told to drop his mistrust and open his heart to raising a child given from the Spirit (1:20). Joseph should not fear taking this woman as his wife, for she had not been unfaithful to him – no matter what it would look like to friends and family (1:20). Marriage is a serious commitment, and faithfulness to that covenant is something God takes seriously. Without this revelation, Joseph *should* have feared. People who can't make it faithfully through an *engagement* are a *ticking bomb* in a marriage, unless God transforms their heart!

Joe was told to reign in his emotions and ego and be obedient to the revealed Word. He could not shape this story – he was to FOLLOW. He was to give up the right to choose the name of the baby – a very great privilege that was well illustrated by Zecharias and John's birth. The future of these sons was NOT in their earthly father's hands – and they needed to surrender that in the beginning of the venture. At the same time, both Joseph and Zecharias got to fill the physical role of naming their sons. Joseph received the privilege of naming the boy according to God's direction (1:21). Even though his role was diminished, he had a role. God didn't cut him out, but loved him enough to include him.

The greatest lesson in the first dream was this: You cannot PREDICT LIFE, you cannot always UNDERSTAND LIFE – but you are called to FOLLOW GOD....Don't overlook the fact that God gave His Son to a man that He could trust to follow instructions! That makes me pause and wonder: What would God entrust to me if He KNEW He could count on me to follow Him through ANYTHING?

In order for Joe to be used by God, he had to "get over" himself. He had to face that God's leading meant that his momentary feelings had to be subservient to God's plan. God was working a plan through the misunderstanding and pain... because God was doing something far bigger than Joe could have imagined.

Lessons from the life of Jesus (1)

Joe was thinking of his family and his leadership in a congregation – both important issues. God was planning to SAVE THE WORLD – a bit more significant. Joe was concerned that his role in God's work might be damaged by things said in relation to this pregnancy – but God was going to give HIM the unique privilege of handling His Son, caring for Him in a way Adam didn't so long ago. Joseph was going to be the first to look at the baby and utter the name "Yeshua" – Savior!

What is God calling on YOU to do that is HARD? What habit is hindering your walk? What ego-driven pursuit is clogging up your walk with God? When you lay your head on your pillow at night, can you see what is keeping you from surrendering your heart to God and following His Word? Are friends telling you, "It's really ok!" – but you KNOW it isn't! It is time to hear from the ancient lesson of Joseph.

The dream matched what God had long before promised. God had shared that the Messiah would come from Bethlehem (Micah 5:2). He told through Daniel the timing of the coming (173,880 days after the command to rebuild Jerusalem in Daniel 9:26ff). He said that He would send one who was "God with us" in Isaiah 7:14. He promised He would bring light to the Galilee highway used by Gentiles in their international travels (Isaiah 9:6). He promised the Messiah as a child, born to His people and that child would be called Wonderful, Counselor, Mighty God, Everlasting Father, Prince of Peace (Isaiah 9:6) as He was when Thomas saw Him after the resurrection and cried out to Jesus in John 20:28, "My Lord and My God!" or when Paul called Jesus both God and Savior (in Titus 2 and 3).

Joseph awoke and followed what the angel told him to do, agreeing to abide to the covenant marriage but not consummating the marriage (1:24-26). Soon a Roman census was announced and Joseph journeyed to Bethlehem (his ancestral home, Lk. 2:1-4) with Mary. The child was born... in the event that Joe wasn't "going to make a big deal about it" – God announced it over the hillside to some noisy nighttime shepherds. I'm sure the birth of Jesus was the worst kept secret in Bethlehem that night!

Time for a SECOND DREAM

Joe stayed on in Bethlehem for the duration of the census. In Rome, Censors were chosen from former Consuls of Rome (Consul was the highest office at the time beside the Emperor). Censors were selected every fifth year and given "Imperium" (the right of command by the Senate of Rome) to conduct a census, then follow it with the giving of contracts for bridges, roads and public works projects. As a result, it appears people in Provinces had their lives routinely disrupted at intervals. Joe was still in Bethlehem well after the baby Jesus became the toddler Jesus – and was visited by some eastern Magi (2:1-12). This "secret" was getting harder to hide – and now Herod the King was involved.

It was about that time that dream number two came along:

Joseph had a second revelatory dream - and this one was not to settle something INSIDE HIM, but rather to help him perceive an oncoming peril. Joe's **family was in danger**, and he needed to move them to Egypt (outside the jurisdiction of Herod the Great) for a time (Matthew 2:13-15). Let's examine the record:

Mt. 2:13 "Now when they had gone, behold, an angel of the Lord appeared to Joseph in a dream and said, "Get up! Take the Child and His mother and flee to Egypt, and remain there until I tell you; for Herod is going to search for the Child to destroy Him." 14 So Joseph got up and took the Child and His mother while it was still night, and left for Egypt. 15 He remained there until the death of Herod. This was to fulfill what had been spoken by the Lord through the prophet: "OUT OF EGYPT I CALLED MY SON."

A second time God stepped in to work on behalf of Joe's family – and to protect Jesus and the Redemption Mission. For Joe, the lesson of trust was deepened. The fact is that Joe was a dad, a husband, and a provider. His living was as a builder, and that work was not helped by all the interruption of forced moves. Rome moved him for a census – and now Herod moved him out of anger and jealousy... but in actuality GOD moved him. The "forced moves" of our lives are often God's *repositioning* to get us to the right place for His plan.

From Joe's perspective, it would be easy for him to conclude that he could not protect his family apart from God's work on his behalf. He couldn't choose to order where they would live. He was called to FOLLOW the One Who knew what he could not know.

The big lesson of the second dream was you CANNOT PROTECT people from life's hardships – even yourself. You are called to FOLLOW GOD and let His protection be your only covering.

THE THIRD AND FOURTH DREAMS CAME

Joe knew that he couldn't PREDICT LIFE, nor could he PROTECT PEOPLE HE LOVED FROM LIFE – he was just following God's direction as God offered it. He moved with the family...Some time passed, and Joe waited as God held his little family in Egypt. The language was strange. The customs were pagan. The place was hotter and more uncomfortable than you can imagine. He probably lived off the gifts of the Magi and waited as his saving sunk lower and lower. His male desire to LEAD had been trimmed – but this was getting old. His male ego based on accomplishment was being badly eroded. The surrender process is never easy on leader types – and many men find following God a difficult thing.

Sometime after the death of Herod the Great, Joseph dreamed a third time. The angel of the Lord told him to bring the baby back to Israel's homeland, and he moved the family back up to Nazareth in the land of Zebulon (Matthew 2:19-23):

Mt. 2:19 "But when Herod died, behold, an angel of the Lord appeared in a dream to Joseph in Egypt, and said, 20 "Get up, take the Child and His mother, and go into the land of Israel; for those who sought the Child's life are dead." 21 So Joseph got up, took the Child and His mother, and came into the land of Israel. 22 But when he heard that Archelaus was reigning over Judea in place of his father Herod, he was afraid to go there. Then after being warned by God in a dream, he left for the regions of Galilee, 23 and came and lived in a city called Nazareth. This was to fulfill what was spoken through the prophets: "He shall be called a Nazarene."

Did you hear those verses? There were ANOTHER TWO DREAMS mentioned...Joe came back to Israel, heard who was on the throne and was afraid *again*. The continuing theme of his life is that he gets afraid – and that fear was matched, step by step with the direction of God's Word. Joseph learned that God didn't need him to be particularly COURAGEOUS... just carefully obedient to God's revealed Word. When Joe followed, that was all the boldness God demanded to use His life for God's glory.

The fact is, that Joe learned that he cannot become IMMUNE to fear and pain – but he could carefully follow God's Word.

Joseph was reported to have died when Jesus was young. He apparently did not live to see Jesus become well known. Yet, his name and character are the stuff of legend. These were HARD lessons: I cannot PREDICT LIFE, I cannot PROTECT PEOPLE FROM LIFE, and I cannot become IMMUNE TO LIFE'S FEARS – but I can follow God's Word.

Let me ask you something: "Do you think he will say in Heaven, 'It was worth it! I obeyed the Lord and it was truly worth it!'" I think Joe will be an eternal testimony to this truth: God will lead you if you surrender to *His* story and not make your life about *your* story!

Jesus said it best: John 12:24 "Truly, truly, I say to you, unless a grain of wheat falls into the earth and dies, it remains alone; but if it dies, it bears much fruit. 25 "He who loves his life loses it, and he who hates his life in this world will keep it to life eternal. 26 "If anyone serves Me, he must follow Me; and where I am, there My servant will be also; if anyone serves Me, the Father will honor him."

Lessons from the life of Jesus (1)

Joe gave up *HIS* DREAM for *GOD'S* DIRECTIONS – but what did he truly LOSE? Nothing… nothing at all. He WAS SIGNIFICANT. He DID make a difference! He played his role for God.

Following His Footsteps:
Lesson Four: "The First Thanksgiving" (Luke 2)

Our nation, despite attempts by more modern historians to suggest otherwise, has a long history of offering thanks to the God of the Bible. In 1621, the Plymouth colonists and Wampanoag Indians shared an autumn harvest feast that is acknowledged today as one of the "first Thanksgiving" celebrations in the colonies. For over two centuries, days of thanksgiving appear to have been celebrated by individual colonies and nascent states, but it wasn't until 1863, amid the Civil War, the weighted President Abraham Lincoln looked at his broken country and proclaimed a national "Thanksgiving Day" to be held each November. It is an increasingly uncomfortable part of our history to the modern secularist – but it endures in the American landscape.

Yet, I would suggest the first thanksgiving in the Bible was not a day of national celebration, but a story of seven people, tied together in a story of celebration of thanks in the face of the news of the birth of the Savior. Yes, the first Christmas was actually the setting of the "first thanksgiving". I am not suggesting no one had ever been thankful before. What I am suggesting is the record of the birth of Jesus was the first structured attempt in the Bible to reflect on a uniform response to God's hand at work in the redemption of the world. Luke is the first author that placed into systematic writing a treatise of thanksgiving – as he reflected on how each person came to recognize what God was doing.

In our last study, we attempted to delve into the Joseph story found in Matthew's Gospel. We noted that both Matthew and Luke recorded genealogies, but after that they seemed very different in their perspectives on the "pre-ministry" they disclosed:

- Matthew focused on how God directed Joseph.
- Luke focused more on thankful responses to the wondrous message that God sent Messiah.

Here is the question we are posing to the text of Luke today: "What does the Scripture tell us was the **proper response** to the coming of Messiah?" The answer is at the heart of our lesson...

Key Principle: The proper response to the Good News of Messiah is thanksgiving and praise, filled with JOY!

Look at the players that are mentioned in Luke and note their responses to the revelation that Messiah was finally coming to the world:

Elizabeth (1:41-43; 45) – representing the longing women of the Jewish world!

Most every woman in the ancient world desired to bear children – because it was the single act that gave them universally understood significance. In some cases in Scripture, as with Leah of old, it was a way to keep a husband's favor. The telling reality of how deeply this was felt is expressed in the woeful weeping of Hannah, mother of the prophet Samuel, before her womb was opened. Elizabeth was clearly among the women who felt "shamed" by her barren state, and because jubilant at the news that God remembered her tears and cries. Six months into her pregnancy, Elizabeth was visited by her cousin, Mary – who was also pregnant. This is the familiar exchange:

Luke 1:41 When Elizabeth heard Mary's greeting, the baby leaped in her womb; and Elizabeth was filled with the Holy Spirit. 42 And she cried out with a loud voice and said, "Blessed [are] you among women, and blessed [is] the fruit of your womb! 43 "And how has it [happened] to me, that the mother of my Lord would come to me? ...45 "And blessed [is] she who believed that there would be a fulfillment of what had been spoken to her by the Lord."

Elizabeth exclaimed words of praise immediately when she saw Mary. They were LOUD praises, according to Luke! She called Mary "blessed", she called the baby inside Mary "blessed" and then made the humblest of remarks. She asked: "Why would someone as important as the mother of my Lord come for a visit to my little home?" Yet her final words were the most significant and encouraging: 45 "And blessed [is] she who believed..." The pregnancy happened TO Mary, but the belief was her choice.

One of the aspects of the JOY of the news that Messiah has come is the continual celebration that reminds a culture and a nation that many have believed, and in believing they found life! We must admit that even *that truth* is quickly becoming a battle for the soul of our nation. I heard from another preacher friend some time ago:

A school teacher in the Midwest was told to remove her "Jesus is the reason for the season" pin when she entered the public school where she taught. She refused and was brought to the school principal, her immediate supervisor. According to her handbook she had the right to speak to the school board at their regularly scheduled meeting in the even that disciplinary measures were pending – and she opted to do so. Before the school board she asked: "What was offensive about the pin?" A school board member said: "This violates the establishment of religion clause of the Constitution – because we are a state-sponsored public institution in a pluralistic country.

The teacher replied: "When, last Autumn, I wore a statement by a Christian minister – Dr. Martin Luther King, Jr.- concerning the inalienable rights of all men given by God for the whole month of black history, no one complained I was promoting Baptist causes. When in the winter I wore on a pin the words of Mother Teresa concerning the call to truly care for the hurting, no one complained that I was promoting Catholicism. When I wore for a whole month the words of Mahatma Gandhi "about peace within shown by peace without", no one thought that I was promoting Hinduism. Why is the simple fact that my pin states that we celebrate a winter holiday in our culture because of the birth of the baby Jesus now considered "an establishment of religion"? Since we teach our students each November that Pilgrims first arrived to allow the free practice of their Christian faith, why is Jesus singled out to be dismissed from public view? The board dismissed her from the meeting with an apology, and she kept the pin on for the duration of the Christmas season.

The modern push to change the memory of our nation belies the truth of why we are here and how we got to be what God made us to become. We have been blessed, and the practice of joyful celebration over the coming of Jesus is one of the opportunities we have to show our faith as tender, human and compassionate. It is a time we can pronounce the goodness of God – not leaving broken man in darkness. Our remembrances of Jesus' birth offer a positive and reinforcing practice that helps us keep our faith in the public eye in America. It is for that reason the observation has come under attack; and it is for that reason we must joyfully and lovingly keep that engagement going!

Baby John (1:44) – representing all unconscious creation!

In that same visit scene, I skipped over the baby John's little tumble in the womb of Elizabeth:

Luke 1:44 "For behold, when the sound of your greeting reached my ears, the baby leaped in my womb for joy.

I see two important applications here, and I hope I am not drifting too far from the text. First, am I stretching the point to say that the coming of Jesus also affects the REST of creation? Consider the words of the Apostle Paul to the Roman believers:

Romans 8:18 For I consider that the sufferings of this present time are not worthy to be compared with the glory that is to be revealed to us. 19 For the anxious longing of the creation waits eagerly for the revealing of the sons of God. 20 For the creation was subjected to futility, not willingly, but because of Him who subjected it, in hope 21 that the creation itself also will be set free from its slavery to corruption into the freedom of the glory of the children of God. 22 For we know that the whole creation groans and suffers the pains of childbirth together until now. 23 And not only this, but also we ourselves, having the first fruits of the Spirit, even we ourselves groan within ourselves, waiting eagerly for [our] adoption as sons, the redemption of our body.

The baby in the manger was the invasion of God from the spiritual world into the physical world. It was part of the battle plan to regain that which was stolen away... but it isn't completed yet. God is taking back His world, but the full redemption of it hasn't happened until He calls for an end to the fight. Those who walk in rebellion look strong in this hour – but they are not equal to His mighty hand. His great patience with men make them think He is unable to silence them – but they are wrong. Creation waits for the completion of redemption, and John's little partially formed body could not hold back from joining the chorus of excitement on behalf of all creation!

Second, not to press the point too far – but is it not ironically true in our day that those who truly believe in Jesus as their Savior represent some of the most ardent advocates for an unborn baby who is yet in the womb?

A literal approach to the Bible yields the sense that God is at work in a child before the time of their delivery and self-sustained life on the planet. The very breath of God is within them as living beings, and God has therefore given them intrinsic worth. I*t is for this reason that believers are so ardently PRO-LIFE. The fact that our GOD became a baby, and was delivered into our world by the means all of us came into it, makes our story unique and compelling – but it also reminds that even the birth process is a created and God-ordained action.

If all creation awaits final redemption, if the fallen and broken systems of this world are anticipating the time when they will be fully free of the effects of the "Fall of mankind", should we not JOYFULLY and THANKFULLY celebrate the reality that Jesus was sent here to save mankind? Must we not press to keep that celebration at the fore of our calendar?

Zacharias (1:67-70) – representing the doubting but now convinced!

We noted in the previous two lessons some thoughts about Zacharias, but it is worth mentioning his role here, because Luke does:

Luke 1:67 And his father Zacharias was filled with the Holy Spirit, and prophesied, saying: 68 "Blessed [be] the Lord God of Israel, For He has visited us and accomplished redemption for His people, 69 And has raised up a horn of salvation for us In the house of David His servant—70 As He spoke by the mouth of His holy prophets from of old...

The celebration of God's goodness at the Advent Season is a renewal that God kept His promises delivered through the prophets. Skeptics attack, but many thinking skeptics are changed by what they see, both in the study of the Scriptures AND in the testimony of those who uphold the truth of the Word! Sir William Ramsey sought to prove Luke an inaccurate historian and ended his days in defense of the Gospel. The sheer weight of the archaeological evidence and geographical detail convinced him. Yet, for Lee Stroebel, it took watching other believers and the way they remembered Christmas.

Lee, a reporter for the Chicago Tribune and a self-professed atheist was sitting at his desk on Christmas Eve. A slow news day he found himself reminiscing about the Delgado family that he had featured while writing a series of articles about Chicago's neediest people a few days earlier. The Delgado's were comprised of a grandmother named Perfecta and her two granddaughters, Jenny age 13 and her sister Lydia 11 years old. He remembered how unprepared he was when he walked into their two room apartment on the west side of Chicago for the interview; bare halls and bare walls, no furniture, no rugs, nothing but a kitchen table and a handful of rice in the cupboards. He learned during the interview that Jenny and Lydia only had one short-sleeved dress apiece, plus a thin gray sweater that they shared. On cold days when the girls walked the half-mile to school, one of the girls would start with the sweater and then give it to the other at the halfway mark. It was all they had. Perfecta wanted more for her granddaughters and would gladly have worked, but her severe arthritis and age made work too difficult and painful. Since it was a slow news day Lee decided to check out a car and drive to Chicago's west side to check up on the Delgado's. When Jenny opened the door he couldn't believe what he saw! His article on the Delgado's had touched the hearts of many subscribers who responded with furniture and appliances, rugs, dozens of coats, scarves and gloves. The girls wouldn't have to share a sweater any longer. There was cartons and cartons and boxes of food everywhere. They had so much food that the cupboards and closets couldn't contain it. Someone had even donated a Christmas tree, and under it were mounds of presents and thousands of dollars in cash! Lee was astonished! But what astonished him the most was what he found Perfecta and her granddaughters doing. They were preparing to give most of it away. "Why would you give so much of this away?" Lee asked. Perfecta responded, "Our neighbors are still in need. We cannot have plenty while they have nothing. This is what Jesus would want us to do." Lee was dumbfounded. After regaining his composure he asked Perfecta another question. He wanted to know what she and the girls thought about the generosity that was shown to them. Again, Lee was not prepared for the answer. She said, "This is wonderful, this is very good." "We did nothing to deserve this; it's all a gift from God. But," she added, "It is not his greatest gift, Lee. No, we celebrate that tomorrow. Jesus." Lee was speechless as he drove back to the office. In the quiet of his car he noted a couple of observations. He had plenty and along with it plenty of anxiety, while the Delgado's despite their poverty had peace. Lee had everything and yet wanted more, but the Delgado's had nothing and yet knew generosity. Lee had everything and yet his life was as bare as the Delgado's apartment prior to the article running. And yet the Delgado's who had nothing were filled with hope, contentment and had a spiritual certainty. Even though Lee had so much more than the Delgado's, he longed for what they had in their poverty. (From a sermon by Bryan Fink "Christmas is for all the Lees/Leighs of the World" 12/25/2008)

Mary (2:10) – representing those to whom God has made a personal promise – and then delivered EXACTLY as He said!

Mary's story is so well known, we need only touch it here:

Luke 2:1 Now in those days a decree went out from Caesar Augustus, that a census be taken of all the inhabited earth. ... 7 And she gave birth to her firstborn son; and she wrapped Him in cloths, and laid Him in a manger, because there was no room for them in the inn...17 When they had seen this, they made known the statement which had been told them about this Child. 18 And all who heard it wondered at the things which were told them by the shepherds. 19 But Mary treasured all these things, pondering them in her heart.

The memory was hard. Mary wasn't accepted by the whole family, and gave birth in the room at the rear of the cave in the three-room cave style home. She listened to the shepherds, and she pondered what God was doing. She would suffer the pain of loss later, but for now she could lay quietly and drift along between thought and sleep... Did not God do exactly as He promised? Yet, in the days to come, the world would make that gift about their own gifts, and that day about everything BUT the Savior that came to rescue a lost mankind.

We shouldn't be surprised... that is what the world does when God shows Himself through the lives of men and women – they shift the subject!

"Valentinus was the name of a young man who lived in Rome during reign of Claudius II (Gothicus) during the third century, when Christians were being persecuted. Though Valentinus did not claim to be a Christian himself, he was instrumental in helping early believers. For that he was imprisoned. From that dank holding cell he surrendered his heart to Jesus Christ and was later condemned to death. He was beaten with clubs, stoned and finally beheaded outside the Flaminian Gate (near modern Piazza del Popolo) on February 14, 269 CE. After his death, this gate was known as Porta Valentini, but that name faded into history. While he was in prison he sent messages to his friends saying, "Remember your Valentine!" and "I love you."

Can you imagine the story moving from God's "agape" love from a believer to "eros" and modern Hallmark cards for lovers? Of course you can. It is what people do with the testimony the church doesn't insist is kept alive in our culture!

Here is the truth: If believers don't hold on to the truths of the events of our faith – the world won't do it for us. The USE our faith to make more products and get more wealth. Those who know what God said must make a priority out of keeping the truths of God's Word a part of our celebrations, and allow the world to observe how these things have changed us.

Shepherds (2:8-20) – representing a caring few!

We can all remember the shepherds and their involvement on that strange night:

Luke 2:8 In the same region there were [some] shepherds staying out in the fields and keeping watch over their flock by night. 9 And an angel of the Lord suddenly stood before them, and the glory of the Lord shone around them; and they were terribly frightened. 10 But the angel said to them, "Do not be afraid; for behold, I bring you good news of great joy which will be for all the people; 11 for today in the city of David there has been born for you a Savior, who is Christ the Lord. 12 "This [will be] a sign for you: you will find a baby wrapped in cloths and lying in a manger." 13 And suddenly there appeared with the angel a multitude of the heavenly host praising God and saying, 14 "Glory to God in the highest, And on earth peace among men with whom He is pleased." 15 When the angels had gone away from them into heaven, the shepherds [began] saying to one another, "Let us go straight to Bethlehem then, and see this thing that has happened which the Lord has made known to us."...

Look at the way the Heavenly army framed the coming of the Savior. They offered a Savior, a sign and a song – and off they went. Did they go with anticipation and joy, or solemnity and sorrow? I think of the words of Charles Haddon Spurgeon:

"It is joy to all nations that Christ is born, the Prince of Peace, the King who rules in righteousness...Beloved, the greatest joy is to those who know Christ as a Savior...The further you submit yourself to Christ the Lord, the more completely you know Him, the fuller will your happiness become. Surface joy is to those who live where the Savior is preached; but the great deeps, the great fathomless deeps of solemn joy which glisten and sparkle with delight, are for such as know the Savior, obey the Anointed One, and have communion with the Lord Himself...you will never know the fullness of the joy which Jesus brings to the soul, unless under the power of the Holy Spirit you take the Lord your Master to be your All in all, and make Him the fountain of your intensest delight."

Simeon (2:28) – representing anxious believing Israel!

On the eighth day, Jesus needed to be named and circumcised. Joseph and Mary took him to the Temple in Jerusalem, where He first shed His blood for the covenant with Abraham.

Luke 2:21 And when eight days had passed, before His circumcision, His name was [then] called Jesus, the name given by the angel before He was conceived in the womb. ... 25 And there was a man in Jerusalem whose name was Simeon; and this man was righteous and devout, looking for the consolation of Israel; and the Holy Spirit was upon him. 26 And it had been revealed to him by the Holy Spirit that he would not see death before he had seen the Lord's Christ. 27 And he came in the Spirit into the temple; and when the parents brought in the child Jesus, to carry out for Him the custom of the Law, 28 then he took Him into his arms, and blessed God, and said, 29 "Now Lord, You are releasing Your bond-servant to depart in peace, According to Your word; 30 For my eyes have seen Your salvation, 31 Which You have prepared in the presence of all peoples, 32 A LIGHT OF REVELATION TO THE GENTILES, And the glory of Your people Israel." 33 And His father and mother were amazed at the things which were being said about Him. 34 And Simeon blessed them and said to Mary His mother, "Behold, this [Child] is appointed for the fall and rise of many in Israel, and for a sign to be opposed—35 and a sword will pierce even your own soul-- to the end that thoughts from many hearts may be revealed."

Imagine standing on the south porch of the Temple that day! You moved into the line at the Mikveh (the ritual bath) and emerged from its chamber with a ticket that said "cleansed". You made your way into the Hulda gates, your ears catching portions of the crowds singing as they entered the Temple of the Lord. Up the stairs you climbed, and onto the open space of the Gentile court. You turned back, and the crowd was gathering around an old man who was prophesying. He was proclaiming that what God said in the PAST WAS COMING TRUE and what God was promising for the future would also be upon them people in the days to come. The celebration of Messiah's coming was seasoned throughout with people who proclaimed God's faithfulness to His prophetic word!

In his book Science Speaks, Peter Stoner applied the modern study of probability to eight prophecies regarding Christ. He offered these words: "The chance that any man might have ...fulfilled all eight prophecies is 1 in 10 to the 17th power. That would be 1 in 100,000,000,000,000,000." (one hundred quadrillion) Stoner suggested by way fo illustration that "we take 10 to the 17th power in number of silver dollars (which we could not do) and lay them on the face of Texas (which we WOULD not do!)... they will cover all of the state two feet deep. If we were to mark one silver dollar and mix the mass thoroughly... and if we were to blindfold a man and tell him he can travel as far as he wishes, but he must pick up [that one marked silver dollar.] What chance would he have of getting the right one?" Stoner concludes, "Just the same chance that the prophets would have had of writing those eight prophecies and having them all come true in any one man,...providing they wrote them in their own wisdom." (Peter Stoner, Science Speaks)_.

Anna (2:38) – representing the people God redirected!

If there was ever a case of God's redirection, it was in the life of Anna. She learned a critical lesson: God may call upon you to reset your personal expectations to be of best use to His service:

Luke 2:36 "And there was a prophetess, Anna (shortened: Channah, or "Grace") the daughter of Phanuel, of the tribe of Asher. She was advanced in years and had lived with her husband seven years after her marriage, 37 and then as a widow to the age of eighty-four. She never left the temple, serving night and day with fastings and prayers. 38 At that very moment she came up and began giving thanks to God, and continued to speak of Him to all those who were looking for the redemption of Jerusalem."

Anna was very old by the time we are introduced to her in the Word. She was widowed after a marriage that lasted only a brief seven years. Now eighty-four years old, Anna learned patience and dependence upon God. She fasted and prayed day and night, never leaving the Temple. She was not like most women of her time. She chose a different path. Instead of finding her identity in a second marriage and raising children – she heard God's direction and went a different way than people expected. She chose to serve the Lord. Her expectations, probably the same as other women of her day, were dramatically altered by God's superintending in her life. She learned to move through the terrible pain of losing her husband, relying on God to financially and emotionally meet the needs of her life.

The people who have encouraged me the most were the people who over the long haul of life have learned to drink from the well of satisfaction from the Lord even when their life circumstances were not ideal. Sixty-five years of waiting is incredible patience to wait for anything – much less a baby to mark the redemption. God is in no hurry! We will not experience instant depth, instant passion, instant deep praise. Genuine change of heart takes time. Genuine weaning of self-satisfaction to God's purposes requires time and a painful transition as I leave the throne of my heart and He takes it.

What if Anna decided not to come in on Tuesdays because she was feeling lazy? What if she accommodated her feelings of disobedience and thought: I don't feel like looking for the Messiah this morning – I will go in latert? The blessings of being obedient far outweigh the temporary satisfaction of placating my wants and desires.

Luke 2:38 At that very moment she came up and began giving thanks to God, and continued to speak of Him to all those who were looking for the redemption of Jerusalem."

Others are defined by their roles – Anna's role was stripped from her and THEN God defined her real purpose. God used her in spite of being the definition of poor and hopeless. She was not forsaken, she was being set up to accomplish her life's purpose!

One after another, the people of Luke's account gave PRAISE to God for what He did in sending His Son! Can we not do the same?

"In the midst of the moral collapse of our generation, can we not ask: "What happened to our JOY as believers?" I recognize the need for sobriety in these days. I see the same news you do. Yet. GOD invaded the planet. His salvation is now freely available – regardless of my background and any of my past failings. I can KNOW GOD, I can WALK WITH GOD... and all of that happened because Jesus put on skin and took my place in the penalty of my rebellion.

He came to set men free! We can hang our long faces as much as we choose to – allowing the enemy to make those who have been set free weep like the world is still bound in chains... but it IS NOT! The Son has come to dispel the darkness, to break the chains, to lift the fallen, to crush the enemy. The Savior has become our Rescuer, and our lives need not be dominated by the momentary issues of the flesh. We CAN celebrate. We SHOULD celebrate. Our world will be nothing but dreary if those set free by Messiah succumb to living like they are still in chains. Truly, the proper response to the Good News of Messiah is thanksgiving and praise, filled with JOY!

Following His Footsteps:
Lesson Five: "The Incredible Shrinking Man" (John 3:22-36)

In 1957, Jack Arnold adapted a novel into a sci-fi movie that was titled: "The Incredible Shrinking Man". The film went on to gain awards in 1958, and was considered by some to be a minor classic in its field. The story was a tale of a businessman who vacationed with his family off the California coast and encountered a strange radioactive cloud that left a sparkled coating on the man's skin. About six months later, the man began to notice he was visibly shrinking. Doctors studied the man and determined the cloud, and a later exposure to an insecticide caused his body to begin to shrink. As he grew smaller, he became famous for his malady, but sunk deeper into a depression. Now very small, he was eventually trapped and attacked in a famous and chilling scene, by his former family pet, a common house cat. Thought to have been killed, he actually escaped into his basement and was forced to navigate its terrors at an ever smaller and smaller size. Much of the time in the basement is spent battling a voracious spider, trying to stem off his own hunger, and facing a lasting fear that he would eventually shrink down to oblivion. Eventually, he escaped the basement, but continued to shrink. He eventually came to terms with his fate and concluded he still "mattered in the universe" because, as he put it, "To God there is no zero." Comforted he faced his future without fear.

Getting smaller is a very real fear to many people – but not in the way the movie was depicting it. They are not afraid of radioactive clouds causing them to be reduced in size – but they do not want to shrink in the eyes of men and women around them. Many are hungry to have, and keep, an impact. They hunger for significance, and fight to remain relevant. As we age, many of us learn enough about ourselves to recognize our own self-protection and our reactions to feeling marginalized.

The truth is this: I must choose to become less significant in myself to have God work through me powerfully. If I contrive and strive to be relevant, my memory will be swept away in short order. This isn't a new idea…

In Yorkshire, England, during the early 1800s, two sons were born to a family named Taylor. The older one set out to make a name for himself by entering Parliament and gaining public prestige. But the younger son chose to give his life to Christ. He later recalled, "Well do I remember, as in unreserved consecration I put myself, my life, my friends, my all, upon the altar. I felt I was in the presence of God, entering into covenant with the Almighty." With that commitment, Hudson Taylor turned his face toward China and obscurity. As a result, he is known and honored on every continent as a faithful missionary and the founder of the China Inland Mission (now known as Overseas Missionary Fellowship). For the other son, however, there is no lasting monument. When you look in the encyclopedia to see what the other son has done, you find these words, "the brother of Hudson Taylor." "…he that doeth the will of God abideth for ever" (1 John 2:17).

What was clear to Hudson Taylor, must become clear to every believer if they are to be powerfully used for God's positive purpose…

Principle: Godly people learn to shrink, allowing the words and work of the Master to displace their own self-importance.

I can think of **no one** who overtly exemplified this truth in the Bible (about shrinking to self) better than the "cousin" of Jesus – John the Baptizer. Before we dig into that truth, let's refresh our memory with a few Biblical details about John:

- First, we know that his birth was announced by the angel Gabriel to Zacharias his father, as we have studied in a previous lesson.

- Second, the Gospels make clear that he prepared the way for Jesus' ministry (Mark 1:2-8; John 1:23) and was, in that way, the promised "Elijah type" from Malachi 4:5 "See, I will send the prophet Elijah to you before that great and dreadful day of the Lord comes. 6 He will turn the hearts of the parents to their children, and the hearts of the children to their parents; or else I will come and strike the land with total destruction.".

- Third, he was an unusual man who grew up in the desert wilderness (Luke 1:80). Matthew 3:4 records a certain eccentricity of John: "Now John himself had a garment of camel's hair and a leather belt around his waist; and his food was locusts and wild honey."

- Fourth, John preached a preparatory message of repentance, baptizing people in the Jordan river (Mark 1:4,5). Along with that, John baptized Jesus at the beginning of Jesus' ministry (though John expressed unworthiness to do so - Matthew 3:13-17).

- Fifth, John wasn't self-effacing, he was humble. John was a man of conviction and was not swayed by popular opinion and openly rebuked the "religiously correct" (of the parties of the Pharisees and Sadducees) telling them that works (fruit) not just words show that they have a repentant heart (Matthew 3:6-10).

- Sixth, Jesus held John in very high regard and said concerning John (see Luke 7:28) "I say to you, among those born of women there is no one greater than John; yet he who is least in the kingdom of God is greater than he."

- Seventh, John was not a superhero – but an ordinary man. In a more "human" story concerning him, at a moment of apparent doubt during his imprisonment, John sent his followers to ask Jesus if He was the "One" (anointed) or if there was another (Luke 7:18-20). Herod put John in prison because he spoke against the Tetrarch's stealing of his brother Philip's wife and other wrong things he had done (Luke 3:19-20). Herod later reluctantly had John beheaded in order to keep a promise he made to his stepdaughter (Matthew 14:1-10).

That set the stage for our study, but we need to spend a few moments looking at what the Gospels record about John's understanding of "shrinking to self"... First, let's establish that John DID understand the concept, and then let's look at what details the Gospel writers offer us to recognize how John got there in his life. That will help us make the journey ourselves...

After Jesus was baptized, and after He began to have a significant following, we read of an incident in John's Gospel that highlighted John's character and his desire to shrink in size behind the Savior:

John 3:22 "After these things Jesus and His disciples came into the land of Judea, and there He was spending time with them and baptizing. 23 John also was baptizing in Aenon near Salim, because there was much water there; and [people] were coming and were being baptized—24 for John had not yet been thrown into prison. 25 Therefore there arose a discussion on the part of John's disciples with a Jew about purification. 26 And they came to John and said to him, "Rabbi, He who was with you beyond the Jordan, to whom you have testified, behold, He is baptizing and all are coming to Him." 27 John answered and said, "A man can receive nothing unless it has been given him from heaven. 28 "You yourselves are my witnesses that I said, I am not the Christ,' but, 'I have been sent ahead of Him.' 29 "He who has the bride is the bridegroom; but the friend of the bridegroom, who stands and hears him, rejoices greatly because of the bridegroom's voice. So this joy of mine has been made full. 30 "He must increase, but I must decrease. 31 "He who comes from above is above all, he who is of the earth is from the earth and speaks of the earth. He who comes from heaven is above all. 32 "What He has seen and heard, of that He testifies; and no one receives His testimony. 33 "He who has received His testimony has set his seal to [this], that God is true. 34 "For He whom God has sent speaks the words of God; for He gives the Spirit without measure. 35 "The Father loves the Son and has given all things into His hand. 36 "He who believes in the Son has eternal life; but he who does not obey the Son will not see life, but the wrath of God abides on him."

Seven Character Traits of a Godly Man

The simple record of the encounter at Aenon near Salim offered a window into John's maturity of heart. Look briefly at the passage what contains John's response to questions, and you will see seven character traits that model a godly man who is ready to shrink before the Lord's greatness and exalt his Savior above himself.

First, there is GODLY CONFIDENCE (3:27):

John stood before his own disciples and answered one who attempted at divisiveness through encouraging envy. "Jesus is gaining more popularity than you, sir!" the man said. John didn't blink. He wasn't upset about being upstaged by another preacher. He soothed the envious hearts of his own disciples with these words – "You get what God gives you!" Out of context, these words could be used for one who was simply hiding laziness, but that wasn't the case! John acknowledged that he served a Sovereign God, and he (like all who follow Him) needed to be content in God's hands. Godly men and women lose their self-confidence and gain a "God confidence"! Self-confidence thrives on human affirmation. God confidence thrives on Heaven's smile revealed by the Spirit within. John was courageously confident about what God had in store for him. I cannot help but smile at Zig Ziglar's comment: "Confidence is going after Moby Dick in a rowboat and taking the tartar sauce with you."

Have you ever watched Olympic sports on TV? Put yourself into that picture. Imagine you are competing and you have done your absolute best, but you have one more time to perform in the competition. Just as you prepare your muscles and your mind, your trainer breaks in with a message: "You have already scored enough points for the gold. No one can catch you. Now go out and do this one for fun!" After thousands of hours of training, hundreds of hours of turning down the foods you most want to eat, conditioning, practicing, disciplining...you will go out on the floor with an excitement. You aren't EARNING the medal, you are ENJOYING the sport. You're DONE competing against others, now you are just working on your craft to hone yourself to do it better. That is a picture of godly confidence.

Second, there is a SENSE OF PURPOSE (3:28).

John made the point that he was not unclear within or in his speaking about who he was and why he spoke. He recognized his purpose and place in life. He was the center – not the quarterback. He would have the ball first, but he would have it only for a moment before it was in the hands of the One Who would determine the rest of the play. He was not to be the center of anyone's universe. Only a mature godly man or woman really grasps this. Though we all have a deep longing to be the center of someone's universe – our place as believers is help others put the Lord at the center – not a relationship with US. Godly men and women answer the question, "Father, what have you made me to be?"

Third, there were expressions of JOY (3:29):

John moved the discussion about Jesus to a "betrothal" and a "wedding" – times of great JOY! John learned the secret of taking JOY in being what God created him to be. He didn't "settle" for his lot in life, he REVELED in the joy of his God-given identity as a "close friend of the groom". No one in the bridal party should distract people from the couple – it is their day! Godly men and women seek to take the joy of the journey on each step with them – the resolute assurance that God has not lost interest in them, nor lost the ability to care for them.

Singer MICHAEL CARD told the story of a man named Joseph who came to Christ out of a Muslim background. One day walking a hot, dusty African road, the man met someone who shared Christ with him. He accepted Jesus as his Savior beside that road and the power of the Holy Spirit overwhelmed him with such joy that the first thing he desired was return and tell his whole village. He walked about, door to door, telling of the cross and the forgiveness for sin. He expected the faces of his neighbors to light up as they encountered this wonderful truth. Much to his amazement they became violent, seized him and held him to the ground while the women beat him with strands of barbed wire. He was dragged and left to die alone in the bush. After a time, he was again conscious and made it to a water hole where he spent days recovering and hiding. He was confused and finally decided that he must have left something out or not told the story correctly. After rehearsing the message he returned. Stood in the circle of huts and began to proclaim Jesus. Again grabbed by men and beaten by women, reopening the wounds that had just begun to heal. He was again dragged while unconscious and left to die. Days later he awoke and determined to go back. This time he was attacked before he even opened his mouth. Before he passed out the last thing he saw was that the women who were beating him had begun to weep. This time he awoke in his own bed, the ones who had beaten him were now trying to save his life. The villagers were challenged by their own hatred, and many came to know Jesus Christ. The man did not come to them to condemn them for not believing, but was compelled to come because he was released from his own sin, and he couldn't contain that!

Fourth, John had the CLARITY (3:30)

One can only have this clarity when they see the truth. He recognized Who the Savior was, and without hesitation he said: "He must increase and I must decrease!" The was the crystal clear sound of a voice that has embraced **TRUTH**. John not only knew who he wasn't – he knew Who the main character WAS in the story. Godly men and women recognize that even what we call "our lives" are not our own. The story is not about US; it is not about God's Son!

A person who calls himself frank and candid can very easily find himself becoming tactless and cruel. A person who prides himself on being tactful can find eventually that he has become evasive and deceitful. A person with firm convictions can become pigheaded. A person who is inclined to be temperate and judicious can sometimes turn into someone with weak convictions and banked fires of resolution . . . Loyalty can lead to fanaticism. Caution can become timidity. Freedom can become license. Confidence can become arrogance. Humility can become servility. All these are ways in which strength can become weakness. Dore Schary, Bits & Pieces, December 9, 1993, pp. 3-4... It is only by connecting our lives to the foundational truth – seeing clearly what God says, that we can take our weaknesses and allow them to become our strength!

This is not small affair. The failure of our nation will come as we disconnect ourselves from the truth that government does not bestow rights – God does. He made us, and we made government. As that truth falls from our classrooms, it falls from our children's hearts. They will be ready for tyranny – and they will even invite it as an expedient answer to some supposed emergency. Connection to God's Word offers protection from God's enemy.

Fifth, there was a simple, noticeable and humble SUBMISSION (3:31):

John answered his disciples' complaints with a straightforward claim that Jesus is Lord from Heaven, and worthy of all submission. No man or woman can ever truly be considered Godly that does not understand submission to the Creator. It doesn't mean we will live every moment with our spiritual knees bowed, but it means that is our GOAL – to serve on earth as God's servants do in Heaven. Angels don't add God to their schedule – He IS their schedule. They don't wonder if they have a better way to pull off life – they KNOW they do not. I tell you the truth: Self-willed and stubborn Christians are doing more to damage the Gospel than atheists ever will.

Sixth, he possessed keen DISCERNMENT (3:32-34):

John claimed that Jesus spoke that which He knew first hand, that is was the absolute truth of the Word of God and that it was infused with the limitless power of the Spirit of God. He *trusted* what Jesus taught, and he had the discernment to see it as truth and label it as such. Godliness presupposes the ability to discern truth from nonsense. No godly man or woman will truly walk as they ought without discernment that acts as a screen to filter out the false and allow the truth to permeate.

"George Hunter contends that the first characteristic of a secular person in the modern world is that he or she is ignorant of basic Christianity. It has been said of the Baby Busters, those born between 1963 and 1977 and the first generation to grow up in a postmodern context, that they lack even the memory of a hope-giving gospel. Today many people outside of the church struggle with the concept of Christ's deity. They think he was a good man, perhaps even a prophet, but not God in human form. Further, seventy-two percent of Americans now deny the existence of absolute truth, and few have confidence in the historical accuracy or ethical authority of the Bible. Two-thirds of the population does not know what John 3:16 refers to, and less than four out of every ten Americans have any idea what the term gospel means. Ten percent believe that the name of Noah's wife was Joan of Arc." - James White, Rethinking the Church, p. 41

I am honestly concerned about how many people are "churched" but not "Bibled". They manage to join programs, listen to sermons, attend conferences and yet don't seem to be growing in their grasp of the Word of God – which is usually the STATED purpose of most of those settings. Without grasping God's Word with discernment, they will be swept into the ever-adapting popular forms of "tolerance morality" which is really cloaked self-will and immorality. Because people call evil good does not make it so – and believers must know the difference. Discernment was never a luxury – but now it will determine survival in a world setting that is increasing in flagrant and egregious sin.

Finally, John had CONTEXT (3:35-36):

He had **UNDERSTANDING** of the broader picture of life and afterlife. His frame of decision making wasn't only about EARTH, but about the reality of HEAVEN and what GOD WAS DOING.

He was not so ego bound that all he could perceive was how everything affected him – life held a bigger picture before him. In this larger window view, what God was calling him to do made *real* sense. John understood that God was from the beginning a God of relationship. He loved, and because of that, it was easy for God the Father to offer authority to the Son. If the <u>Father</u> could do that, so could <u>John</u>! He loved Jesus, so surrendering crowds and accolades to Him was not a sacrifice he couldn't accept!

That understanding is where the great truth was revealed from John's lips. Because John saw that the Father in Heaven loved the Son, and trusted the Son completely - John could follow suit and give up any position, title, fame or importance to Jesus. God - out of love - gave the Son authority, how could John give less than his passing fame? He knew that Jesus' coming wasn't just a political stunt or an earthly religious control play.
I cannot find the statement, but in my memory it should be ascribed to John Piper. Years ago I heard it, and it stuck with me (I am adapting as memory serves)…

"What other religion do you know that shares the love of God by that very powerful and majestic being coming to die for a rebel? What other personality claimed openly to be God and died for that claim, yet have millions that follow Him? Buddha never made such a claim. He didn't say he came from God, nor that he was God. Mohammed never made the claim that he was God in human skin – only that he was a prophet that died and remains in the tomb like all other men. In every other religion the word of God is a verbal revelation, a book or a set of moral codes. Only in Christianity does God become flesh. Only in our Savior does He subject Himself to wicked men to win their hearts." (adapted from unknown author).

John recognized the sacrifice of God, and he made his own sacrifice to God…

On March 5, 1994, Deputy Sheriff Lloyd Prescott was teaching a class for police officers in the Salt Lake City Library. During a break he stepped into the hallway, and as he did he saw a gunman forcing 18 hostages into a nearby room. Prescott, who was dressed in street clothes, fell in line with the group and became the nineteenth hostage. The gunman had not noticed him, and Prescott followed them into the room, and shut the door. The gunman announced the order in which hostages would be executed, and then it was that Prescott identified himself as a police officer. A fight ensued, and Prescott, in self-defense, shot the gunman. All of the hostages were released unharmed. The officer placed himself at great risk, but he was not thinking of himself, he was thinking about the danger the hostages were in. (sermon central illustrations).

Why would the Officer Prescott do that? The answer is simple: He thought of another **first**. He shrunk, and they grew. So did John, and it wasn't philanthropy, it was surrender to Jesus.

Godly people learn to shrink, allowing the words and work of the Master to displace their own self-importance.

If you ever get the opportunity to go to Florence in Italy – do it. Near the Ponte Vecchio is a church called Santa Felicia. One piece of artwork in that church was painted by Antonio Ciseri in 1863 called "The Martyrdom of the Seven Maccabees". It recalled a story from 2 Maccabees 7, when about 160 years before Jesus, a tyrant general tried to make seven sons of one woman eat pork. One after another the boys were horribly killed in front of their mother, yet she did not tell them to capitulate – because she taught them to observe the Law of Moses. Faced with the loss of all of her sons, she would not relent – nor would they… What kind of person stands up to pressure like that? The kind that is convinced that following God is more important than physical life itself. "Too radical!" you say? It may seem so. Yet, if we are not willing to stand for God's word, but try to tolerate and compromise our way through – we will have loved this life and lost our opportunity to show Jesus to others when it really counted.

Following His Footsteps:
Lesson Six: "Starting Block" (Matthew 4:1-11; Mk. 1:12-13 and Lk. 4:1-13; John 2:19-51)

I am no sprinter, and I have never won a foot race on any track, anywhere – at least that I can recall. Like most of you, I am a sports *fan* – but I am no sports *man*. As such, I watch the athleticism of younger men and women, and feel the absolute right to comment on their technique as I watch – though I couldn't begin to fathom the sacrifice involved in their preparation, nor would my body be able to do any of my suggested moves were I in their place. As a fan of many sports and a master of exactly *none* – I offer this amateur observation that I have observed: **The race is often determined in the moment after the starting gun.** The right positioning on the "starting block" often proves to be a supreme advantage. Getting started with strength and stability seems, at least from the view from my cushioned recliner (watching on television) an essential step toward winning. **It seems that beginning well is important**. It isn't *everything*, but it is *significant*. Yet, I am not thinking primarily about sports…In our lesson I am thinking about how the earth ministry of Jesus began.

The earthly ministry of our Savior as recorded in the Gospels took place over two thousand years ago, and lasted a mere three to four years long. During that time, Jesus became popular and selected His disciples. I marvel that God's invasion of His fallen planet was pressed into a few short years and took place in one small area of the globe - on a planet in one corner of one galaxy – yet His work is transforming the whole cosmos. What began as a work of human rescue and salvation, will not see its completion until the final transformation when all things that are made new. Our question to consider is this: "How did Jesus begin His ministry?" What were the very **first moments** of God's reclamation of creation like? How did that *beginning* offer a portent of the whole ministry? In the simplest terms, the early record of Jesus' ministry emphasized three aspects of ministry that would dominate the whole work…

Key Principle: The work of ministry is about three things: God's call – selecting us for His work, the enemy's obstruction – attempting to distract us from the assignment and the prime objective of building disciples in the midst of the battle.

Yes, we are referring to the opening of the ministry of Jesus. At the same time, the ministry we have been given is a continuation of the same priorities. We need not redeem man, but the message of that completed redemption IS in our hands, empowered by His Spirit. The record of the opening of Jesus' ministry will help us define three issues:

- What is required to begin a work for God?
- What resistance should we expect when we begin to work out our ministry?
- What is the chief focus of ministry?

When I use the term "ministry", I am not thinking in some professional sense, but in this way: "Ministry is using God's power to accomplish God's purpose in God's way, according to God's stated priorities." Ministry is the LIFE of the follower of Jesus. We have the incredible privilege to live in service to Jesus – and to serve Him by serving others. Let's look into the passages that share how Jesus began the work.

The Presentation of Jesus (Matthew 3:13-17; Mk. 1:9-11 and Lk. 3:21-23)

In the story of the beginning of Jesus' ministry, He was announced as the Deliverer at His baptism in the Jordan by His cousin John. As we look at the scene, ask yourself this question: "What is required to begin a life of service to our Father in Heaven?" In the case of Jesus, His ministry began with a CALL that acted in His case as a public endorsement – so that a handful of those who would follow Jesus had a stunning awakening to His presence. It was a shocking, verbal affirmation from Heaven:

Matthew 3:13 Then Jesus arrived from Galilee at the Jordan [coming] to John, to be baptized by him. 14 But John tried to prevent Him, saying, "I have need to be baptized by You, and do You come to me?" 15 But Jesus answering said to him, "Permit [it] at this time; for in this way it is fitting for us to fulfill all righteousness." Then he permitted Him. 16 After being baptized, Jesus came up immediately from the water; and behold, the heavens were opened, and he saw the Spirit of God descending as a dove [and] lighting on Him, 17 and behold, a voice out of the heavens said, "This is My beloved Son, in whom I am well-pleased."

It is clear in the text that the baptism by John was God the Father's announcement that Jesus had prepared well for the work to come, and that He was ready to commence His redemptive work. Yet, that was admittedly a unique feature that was designed for Jesus. Should I anticipate that God will open Heaven and make such a display for me as I begin to serve Him? No! Yet, there is an example here we should observe that is instructive for us…

First, notice in Matthew 3:13 that Jesus recognized the work God was already doing, and went to John's baptism site. He didn't forge off on His own, but began with a place that God was already moving in hearts, and where God's Word was already being represented. Ministry and service for God isn't about you "doing it all right on a path of your own". Your call to ministry adds you to a team that has already been at work. You are JOINING A TEAM, not establishing the beginning of God's work on earth. I am concerned about those who view themselves as so self-important they cannot place themselves in a position of "team" at all.

Second, John's response to Jesus in Matthew 3:14 reminds us of the kind of ministry we should seek out when we want to be a part of God's work on a team – a ministry that acknowledges the supremacy of Jesus. We need to expect ministry to do more than good works for helpless people. Pagans can fill soup bowls. We need to recognize that real ministry exalts Jesus, and recognizes His unique position as the Eternal Son of God. Good works are important but proper worship at the center of any ministry is essential for those works to have the right meaning.

Third, Matthew 3:15 reminds us that a proper ministry follows the Word of God. John's thoughts were reverent but Jesus' commands were Biblical. Jesus called the play, and John executed it as called – because that is what ministry is supposed to do. We go where Jesus points.

Finally, an essential point for our call to ministry is this: God sets us aside to do the work He gives us. It begins with His affirmation. Because Matthew 3:16-17 are so unique to Jesus, it is easy to obscure this point. I am not suggesting that God will open Heaven for us before a host of our friends and exclaim that we are called to do a work for Him. What I am saying is this: God will affirm your careful preparation, and God will call you to accomplish things for Him if you open yourself to His desires. **The most frustrated believer is one who has a sense of duty without knowledge of God's calling**. God waits to be asked, and waits to be wanted.

Jesus began by going to where God was already working - a place where the Word of God was being explained and the priority of God was being fleshed out. He stood in the water and God affirmed the beginning of His earth ministry in a formal way. You may not see a light from Heaven, but if you yield the balance of your life to your Heavenly Father – He will acknowledge that in your life. He will show it to others. He will affirm that you are following His call.

The story is told of a time when Henry Ford was riding through the Michigan countryside and happened upon a man who was beside the road trying to get his "Model T" working again. The problem was not severe, but the man had no earthly idea how to get it working properly. Ford pulled over his car and jumped out of the driver's seat. He asked the man if he could help. The man was very open to assistance, and Ford had the car purring in minutes. "What a miracle worker you are!" exclaimed the man. "Not really", said Ford. "I am the designer of the automobile, so I know how it works."

Lessons from the life of Jesus (1)

That makes obvious sense to anyone who hears of the story. Yet, think about it: People spend their lives searching for answers to make life work, but won't take their broken lives to the Designer of life. If you do – expect more than restoration – expect a mission. Expect a call. God starts at the point that we surrender to Him – and then He moves us into things we NEVER could have imagined.

Ministry ("using God's power to accomplish God's purpose in God's way, according to God's stated priorities") begins with our surrender and God's affirming call… but that is just the beginning.

By the way, was God's affirmation from Heaven recognized as an important event years after? Yes, indeed! Hebrews 1 opened with the argument of Jesus' position based on that day:

Hebrews 1:1 God, after He spoke long ago to the fathers in the prophets in many portions and in many ways, 2 in these last days has spoken to us in His Son, whom He appointed heir of all things, through whom also He made the world…5 For to which of the angels did He ever say, "YOU ARE MY SON, TODAY I HAVE BEGOTTEN YOU"? And again, "I WILL BE A FATHER TO HIM AND HE SHALL BE A SON TO ME"?

Jesus went to the right place with the right heart and right preparation – but God exalted Him and marked His life. You are not the Redeemer – but God will do the same for you. If you offer Him your life, He will affirm your choice, empower your work and attract others to you. That is the beginning place for your work to accomplish His purposes. When you do that, however, be warned… the complications of life are about to hit you…

The Problem for Jesus (Matthew 4:1-11; Mk. 1:12-13 and Lk. 4:1-13)

Affirmation and accomplishment are exciting to talk about, but they come at a price. God affirms and Satan attacks. If you have walked with God, I need say little about this to you. Let me address the one who is at the beginning of their road of surrendered heart and accomplished ministry. Look carefully at the words that mark out the work of TEMPTATION in our lives:

Matthew 4:1 Then Jesus was led up by the Spirit into the wilderness to be tempted by the devil. 2 And after He had fasted forty days and forty nights, He then became hungry. 3 And the tempter came and said to Him, "If You are the Son of God, command that these stones become bread." 4 But He answered and said, "It is written, MAN SHALL NOT LIVE ON BREAD ALONE, BUT ON EVERY WORD THAT PROCEEDS OUT OF THE MOUTH OF GOD.'" 5 Then the devil took Him into the holy city and had Him stand on the pinnacle of the temple, 6 and said to Him, "If You are the Son of God, throw Yourself down; for it is written, HE WILL COMMAND HIS ANGELS CONCERNING YOU'; and 'ON [their] HANDS THEY WILL BEAR YOU UP, SO THAT YOU WILL NOT STRIKE YOUR FOOT AGAINST A STONE.'" 7 Jesus said to him, "On the other hand, it is written, YOU SHALL NOT PUT THE LORD YOUR GOD TO THE TEST.'" 8 Again, the devil took Him to a very high mountain and showed Him all the kingdoms of the world and their glory; 9 and he said to Him, "All these things I will give You, if You fall down and worship me." 10 Then Jesus said to him, "Go, Satan! For it is written, YOU SHALL WORSHIP THE LORD YOUR GOD, AND SERVE HIM ONLY.'" 11 Then the devil left Him; and behold, angels came and [began] to minister to Him.

Look at the pattern – because it will become familiar if you follow God:

First, don't ignore that temptation came while Jesus was led by the Spirit – it cannot be avoided by a walk with God because it is *part* of the walk (4:1a). We will pass into tempting situations and experiences. God will not forsake us, but He will not block all temptation from coming our way. He will do so at strategic times to protect us – and then expect we will use the armor He provided (Eph. 6:10-20) for the other times. God expects a believer to be wise, prepared and disciplined in areas of temptation.

Second, though not all temptation is directly from the enemy, it all originates with him and can be linked to his person and attitude of rebellion (4:1b). The devil isn't interested in rebelling alone. He wants a degraded audience, destroying their lives beside him. He is at work in our day, "the prince of the power of the air" warping our world's sense of justice to defend perversion as a right and convenience killing as a social necessity. He is laughing as we indulge in entertainments that enrich our rebellion while proclaiming Jesus as our Savior. He is very much behind the things tugging you away from a surrendered heart before God.

Temptation is most effective when we are at a position of need and in a state of dormancy (4:2). Matthew recorded in some detail the specific instance of the temptation of Jesus by His enemy – so that we would learn the pattern:

The tempter began by questioning truth ("if you are the Son of God") and raising Jesus' attentiveness to His own hungry desires ("turn these stones to bread"). This was a call to self-absorbed thinking – focusing more on a desire or need than on careful obedience to His Father.

Here is the great tragedy of America. When the post mortem is done on how the west fell, it will show, I am confident, that a paganization of education was at the core of the fall. Instead of using God's Word as the foundation of truth – we have deliberately replaced the truth with unending questions and bold assertions that such truths do not really exist. As we quadruple our social services budgets and clog the system with an unending number of dysfunctional people, we will see the error of that way. People cannot get life together when they don't have a truth foundation to put it on. When any nation is taught to focus on fulfilling their desires without the balancing truth of taking joy from wholly serving their Creator – they lose their way.

The second phase of the tempter's work attempted to draw the Master into "proving" to the enemy His rightful position while using "half-truths" and "partial quotes" of the Word to do so. This was a call to self-reliant thinking – focusing more on one's position and ability than on the pleasure of our Heavenly Father with our lives.

Here the enemy didn't want to change WHO Jesus was, but rather try to focus Jesus on Himself rather than on His Father – for Whom the whole mission was conceived. Jesus was here for His Father's joy – and focus on Who He is was a distraction from that chief end. Satan is a master at pulling our eyes from the MOST IMPORTANT to the LESSER THINGS – and once our eyes are following his prompting, he will pull our attention into rebellion. Jesus would have none of it. Even as the Eternal Son of God – He knew His call was to serve His Father, and keep His attention on that as His chief joy.

I wonder how many believers have been trained to think this way. Have we really instilled in those we disciple that the chief end of man is to glorify God and enjoy Him in the process? The message of modern Christianity often sounds like the tempter's voice: "Come to Jesus and YOU will find fulfillment and happiness." Even though the words are true, can we not see that they beckon us to get Jesus for our own purposes – and not to surrender our lives to HIS? We must be careful about this, for how we motivate people will show up later in the discipleship process.

The third phase of the temptation was all about exaltation and glory ("cast Yourself down from here") – the enemy offering promised results. When Satan cannot get us to succumb to some warped version of self-desire, when he cannot delude our thinking with half-truths – he will beckon to a deep desire within us to be important and famous. He will summon us to do something that calls for the obvious recognition of our own importance. This is a call to our self-important thinking – focusing on glory for self and not glory for our Father.

I strongly believe we are living in a day of delusion -even within the community of the Christian faith. Many begin with the flawed foundational idea that God's chief interest is their happiness (not holiness). Because of that, anything that would curtail their ability to express their inner desires and feelings could not be commanded by this "reshaped" god they now follow. If they feel they were "made with certain desires", they cannot imagine a god that would tell them to deny their feelings – because their true god is their appetite. We live in a time where even believers have been subtly convinced that the center of the universe is how they feel, not Who they serve – and that separates the modern church from the message of its past.

This can sound harsh, but I truly mean every word of it in love, and it is a pleading question, not to the world, but to my friends who claim to follow Jesus: "What difference does it make "what you feel attracted to" if it conflicts with the Word of God?" Why would I spend my time trying to carefully dissect and discern my feelings instead of simply asking what the Master has said will please Him? Is not greater sacrifice the platform for greater joy in the time of reward? Are we not told to be like Jesus Who surrendered His desires, blessings and comforts to serve His Father's end? With that in mind…Does not God have the right to call you to celibacy if he chooses? Can He not call you to childlessness – regardless of what you feel you desire? When did God give up being in charge of His own plan? Self-centered Christianity isn't Christianity at all – it is a religion cloaked immature selfishness – and we need to see it for the bankruptcy it is.

The attempt Satan used has been a successful method against many. While ineffective against Jesus, the record offers us an ability to know in advance the enemy's way of pulling us off track. It is a model… and we must watch for appeals to self-absorption, self-reliance and self-importance. On each are the fingerprints of a fallen angel.

Jesus answered the tempter's melody with three responses from God's revealed Word: In Matthew 4:4 Jesus faced the tempter and made the simple point that it is God's Word - not man's hunger - that is supreme. What a statement! Jesus literally said that what was more important than what He wanted at that moment (something to eat and drink) was subservient to the Word of God. That is Christian thinking put succinctly and powerfully. His Word moves me to place second my desires. My life here is about sowing; my life to come in Heaven is about reaping. When I get that truth confused I expect people here to be fair, and circumstances here to work out to my benefit. Sometimes they do, and that confuses my focus all the more. Yet, when I live for the eventual applause of Heaven, I gain peace amid the problems on earth. I drop my need for things to please ME, because I want ultimately to please HIM.

Jesus made clear the issue wasn't simply what we DO, but for WHOSE GLORY we do it (Mt. 4:7). A man who lives to make himself happy doesn't live for God's glory... period. When I live for my Master, I can and WILL enjoy life – but that cannot become the goal or I am changing the essential message and purpose of my faith.

In the last retort of Jesus to His enemy (Mt. 4:10) the Master made clear that there comes a time when the best we can do is dismiss temptation with the Word and move on – reasoning with deception is often a lost cause. The attack of the enemy was activated when God acknowledged that Jesus' work of redemption was underway. We should expect nothing less. When we move ahead, the enemy dispatches those who push us back. They may come in the form of temptation to do wrong, or simply temptation to lose focus on the goal.

Here is the point: If we surrender we will be called. When we are called, we will face attack. Yet, there is more. We must understand the priority of ministry or we will spend our lives on the wrong effort – a great many have over the years!

The Priority of Jesus (John 1:29-51)

John 1:29 The next day he saw Jesus coming to him and said, "Behold, the Lamb of God who takes away the sin of the world! ... 35 Again the next day John was standing with two of his disciples, 36 and he looked at Jesus as He walked, and said, "Behold, the Lamb of God!" 37 The two disciples heard him speak, and they followed Jesus. 38 And Jesus turned and saw them following, and said to them, "What do you seek?" They said to Him, "Rabbi (which translated means Teacher), where are You staying?" 39 He said to them, "Come, and you will see." So they came and saw where He was staying; and they stayed with Him that day, for it was about the tenth hour. 40 One of the two who heard John [speak] and followed Him, was Andrew, Simon Peter's brother. 41 He found first his own brother Simon and said to him, "We have found the Messiah" (which translated means Christ). 42 He brought him to Jesus. Jesus looked at him and said, "You are Simon the son of John; you shall be called Cephas" (which is translated Peter)..."

Jesus left the tempter behind and fully fixed his gaze on the mission ahead. It was clear that mission was not simply about the crowds – though it included public ministry. His was a ministry of DISCIPLE MAKING. This was His initial priority, and based on the record of His final hours before the Cross – it was His CENTRAL priority. We must recognize this! The church is not primarily about preserving the culture – it is about replicating disciples that can live truth REGARDLESS of what the culture does.

Disciples came to Jesus because another follower (John) pointed out Jesus to them (John 1:29). If John was concerned with his own fame, he may have hid Jesus from his own followers – and many so called "Christian" leaders do that. They make disciples increasingly dependent upon them – not equipping them and encouraging them to carry the work. They will create ministry based on paid staff, instead of igniting and encouraging the work of the Spirit from the church pew. They will not bring people to MATURITY, but to DEPENDENCE. We must make every effort to do the work of equipping, and keep pointing people to God and His Word – and not to us.

How do you know when disciples are grown? When they are reproducing – when they are calling others to Jesus they are BEGINNING the process. That isn't the end. Having babies doesn't make you a parent – just a biologically functioning adult. Raising children is what makes one a parent. Don't see John 1 as the END, but the beginning of making disciples that make disciples – a subject we will handle more deeply in coming lessons...

Here is the truth of our lesson: The work of ministry is about three things: God's call – selecting us for His work, the enemy's obstruction – attempting to distract us from the assignment and the prime objective of building disciples in the midst of the battle.

According to Mike Neifert in his writing called "Light and Life" (February 1997), staff members from the Bridger Wilderness Area in Wyoming reported receiving comment cards from visitors to their rustic wilderness park:

- Trails need to be reconstructed. Please avoid building trails that go uphill.
- Too many bugs and leeches and spiders and spider webs. Please spray the wilderness to rid the areas of these pests.
- Please pave the trails...Chair lifts need to be in some places so that we can get to wonderful views without having to hike to them.
- The coyotes made too much noise last night and kept me awake. Please eradicate these annoying animals.
- A small deer came into my camp and stole my jar of pickles. Is there a way I can get reimbursed? Please call...
- Escalators would help on steep uphill sections.
- A MacDonald's would be nice at the trailhead.
- Too many rocks in the mountains.

Larry Sarver wrote a sermon that is included in the Sermon Central library on the subject of discipleship and he cited these complaints. I appreciated his insight, so I close with his words:

"These comments and complaints indicate that the people who made them do not really understand what it means to stay in a "wilderness area." They were looking for something convenient and comfortable, but not truly a wilderness experience. In a similar way, many people today do not understand what it means to be a genuine Christian. There are multitudes that often follow Jesus or claim to be a Christian but they do so on their terms and not his. They do not truly comprehend the biblical definition of discipleship. Because of this ignorance there are many who consider themselves to be followers of Jesus who are not, even though in many ways they do look like followers of Jesus. They go to church, have a profession of faith, read their Bibles, pray, even give in the offering, but they are not the real deal or at least are not living and thinking like the real deal. ... there is no reason for anybody to be ignorant or self-deceived... To be a disciple of Jesus you must be committed to him above everything else... In our hearts Jesus must come before our loved ones, self-interest, possessions, careers, hobbies, goals in life, and even our very lives. In practice this commitment to Jesus will be tested and sometimes, in a moment of weakness, Jesus will not come first in our choices, but genuine disciples have made a sincere commitment in their hearts and will not continue to put other things before Jesus." (Adapted from Sermon Central illustrations).

Following His Footsteps:
Lesson Seven: "Exposing the Secret" (John 2)

There are English expressions that are used by various movements in different times in history, and along the way they adapt in meaning. The phrase "*out of the close*t" was used by advertisers long before it was adopted by modern social action groups. More recently, as a surprise to virtually no one, this phrase has become the mantle of those who see themselves as "*bravely stepping forth on issues of sexual preference orientation*". Yet, the phrase actually denotes **exposing a long held secret**. It was historically linked to the idea of "*skeletons in the close*t" – and denoted potentially embarrassing things kept hidden from view out of potential shame. I want to go in **a different direction** with the phrase as we tackle the next part of the ongoing series to follow the footsteps of our Master as we study the record of His life in the Gospels. I want to talk about how a secret identity of Jesus became publicly exposed.

Think of it this way... **Jesus had a secret**. His mother Mary knew what it was because an angel named Gabriel told her thirty years before. His stepfather Joseph knew it, because God told him in dreams thirty years before our story. The angels knew it, because they made the announcement at His birth. The enemy knew it, because he faced Jesus in a "temptation sparring match" in the Wilderness of Judea a short time before the events of today's lesson took place. Yet the truth is that although many *BEINGS* in Heavenly places knew Who Jesus was - the Eternal Son of God living in human flesh –few *PEOPLE* who lived near Him knew the truth of Jesus' identity. This lesson is about how Jesus stepped out of the shadows and showed Himself to be the fulfillment of God's promise from centuries before... man's Redeemer was eating breakfast next door to someone who was clueless of His presence!

The passage for study is John 2, and it offers two essential lessons that set up the **first steps of Jesus' public ministry** after His baptism by John in the Jordan River and after the temptation wrestling match was completed in the nearby Judean

Wilderness. Jesus picked up His first five "would be" disciples, and then two stories unfolded:

- The **first public miracle** of Jesus (John 2:1-11). Jesus turned water into wine at a Cana wedding feast and showed that the ordinary could become the extraordinary – if it received the touch of the Master.

- The **first public challenge** by Jesus (John 2:12-25). Jesus walked into His Father's Temple distracted by the commercial barkers and turn a bazaar into chaos while He showed that much becomes little – when God "weighs in" on religious nonsense.

Key Principle: Jesus knew His place, and revealed it from the very beginning of His public ministry. What He met was resistance, because people want a Rescuer, but not a Master.

It is important that we recognize this truth – because among those who do not both **carefully study the narrative** *and* **believe it is historically valid** – a common notion is that Jesus "slowly discovered" His place as the Son of God. Some "scholars" even express the notion that Jesus was *never* fully aware of it until after the Resurrection. In the more liberal circles of "Christian" thought, that is not even a debated concept – it has been accepted.

Not to pluck a phrase from our current political Benghazi discussion of our current news cycles, but **here is the question of our lesson**: "What did Jesus know and when did He know it?" We are *not* entertaining the debate that Jesus was NOT the Savior – that debate is simply answered by a faithful study of the Gospel accounts that were NOT fuzzy on such things...Our thoughts concern the challenge that Jesus was a benevolent and hapless rabbi that was unaware of some greater position He had. Does the Gospel reveal that? Not at all...

It is **true** that the Bible **does not overtly state the moment at which Jesus knew that He was the Eternal Son of God** sent to die as the "Spotless Lamb" for man's sin. It is also true that He DID know those things. We read that *later* in His ministry Jesus fully expressed Who He was from eternity past, declaring: "Jesus said to them, "Most assuredly, I say to you, before Abraham was, I AM." (John 8:58). Later, John recorded Jesus praying this way: "And now, O Father, glorify Me together with Yourself, with the glory which I had with You before the world was." (John 17:5). Clearly, if the Gospel record is true – Jesus knew His place. Our question is when did Jesus fully grasp that truth?

Some believers want to believe that He was consciously spinning planets while lying in a manger in Bethlehem – a view that I do not hold. Scripture does express that as a young child He was fully aware of His work, but He did feel an early need to be preparing as a boy to complete a work His Father in Heaven sent Him to complete by age 13. On a boyhood trip to the Temple in Jerusalem, Jesus was "sitting in the midst of the teachers, both listening to them and asking them questions." (Luke 2:46). When his parents discovered Him there, He offered this question: "Did you not know that I must be about My Father's business?' But they did not understand the statement which He spoke to them." (Luke 2:49-50). Luke made sure that in reading the account and reader would know that Jesus possessed information beyond what His parents could grasp. After the recorded incident, Luke noted: "And Jesus increased in wisdom and stature, and in favor with God and men" (Luke 2:52). Let me suggest that though Jesus may well have known Who He was, his physical immaturity still lacked the completed ability to make all things clear to those around Him. He needed to grow physically, emotionally and mentally. Though He was cognizant by that time that He was fully God, He needed to become fully a man. Over the early centuries of Christianity, this subject was explored deeply and hotly debated by Church Fathers who were trying to understand the theology of the God-man.

Let's accept the Biblical record that Jesus knew years and years before everyone else understood His mission and move forward with the story. What happened at the early stage of His ministry, then, concerned exposing the truth to those both near to Him and those in charge of the God's people. The two episodes found in John 2 effectively do just that – and then they expose the way people responded to the message that God wanted to both SAVE then and RULE their lives. The first message is preached, loved and celebrated. The second truth (that of the rule of Jesus) is taught seldom and loved little – even by people who profess to follow Jesus. Somehow we have invented in modern Christianity a Sovereign Lord that leads us by following after our desires. That Jesus isn't the one pictured in the Gospels.

First Miracle at Cana

We open the chapter with our first look at the miracle ministry of Jesus:

John 2:1 On the third day there was a wedding in Cana of Galilee, and the mother of Jesus was there; 2 and both Jesus and His disciples were invited to the wedding. 3 When the wine ran out, the mother of Jesus said to Him, "They have no wine." 4 And Jesus said to her, "Woman, what does that have to do with us? My hour has not yet come." 5 His mother said to the servants, "Whatever He says to you, do it." 6 Now there were six stone waterpots set there for the Jewish custom of purification, containing twenty or thirty gallons each. 7 Jesus said to them, "Fill the waterpots with water." So they filled them up to the brim. 8 And He said to them, "Draw [some] out now and take it to the headwaiter." So they took it [to him]. 9 When the headwaiter tasted the water which had become wine, and did not know where it came from (but the servants who had drawn the water knew), the headwaiter called the bridegroom, 10 and said to him, "Every man serves the good wine first, and when [the people] have drunk freely, [then he serves] the poorer [wine]; [but] you have kept the good wine until now." 11 This beginning of [His] signs Jesus did in Cana of Galilee, and manifested His glory, and His disciples believed in Him.

John made clear:

- On the third day there had been a wedding at Cana, and Jesus' mother was there (2:1).
- Jesus and His first five followers were invited (2:2) apparently arriving at the end of the feast.
- When the wine ran out, Mary called upon Jesus to address the problem (2:3), explaining they had run out of wine. She was evidently confident that Jesus was able to meet the need in some incredible way.
- Over Jesus' initial objections (2:4), she left Him with the servants and instructed them to follow all His directions (2:5).
- Jesus told the servants to take the six stone pots that held twenty to thirty gallons each and fill them with water (a stunning violation of their purpose of ritual purity collection – 2:6-7).
- Jesus then told them to draw out from the stone jars a cup and take it to the head cupbearer of the feast and have him sample it for the guests (2:8).
- The cupbearer was shocked and complimented the groom on his surprising stash of excellent wine (2:9-10).

While it is nice to know that Jesus liked weddings, and that Jesus would make a good vintner, why would such an event become important enough to record for posterity?

First, it is important that we understand that Jesus wasn't so "other worldly" that He wouldn't celebrate a wedding with two people starting a new family – His earth ministry wasn't just about lofty theological debates and Satan hunting... it was about loving people and celebrating the stages of their lives with them. Though life is PRIMARILY about the eternal things – life here is a gift from God to be enjoyed, celebrated... it is to be lived. God is nowhere more present than in the room of people who love Him and each other and are falling on the floor laughing hysterically over something that won't let go of their funny bone. God isn't a prude. Anything you have ever enjoyed – He thought of. Any flavor you have ever savored – He created. Any beauty that has ever taken your breath away – He pulled out the brush an painted on the landscape. God is not just powerful and Majestic – He is personal and creative. He knows good coffee and can delight in the swirls of freshly stirred caramel sauce.

Don't you DARE make Him into some monastic prior with itchy clothing eating bread and water! There is no pleasure without the Creator of all things. Even in our fallen state, God's joys still shine through. Let's say it clearly: Jesus knows how to party!

Beyond that truth, we observe in the passage the truth that Jesus speaks, and the ordinary becomes the extraordinary. God isn't into the light adjustment business – He is a total and complete transformer! When Jesus spoke forgiveness over your life, you began a transformation that is ongoing. You know the problems, and you encounter your own resistance – but let's be honest... YOU KNOW YOU ARE BEING CHANGED. You don't want all the things of the world you once did. Your tastes buds are already starting to salivate when you smell the fresh baked bread of Heaven. When people are really in a walk with Jesus – they don't have to be convinced of transforming power – they are living it. Here is the really neat thing: someday soon the Heaven's will open, the trumpet will sound, and the very molecules of my body will be transformed from earth's smell of slow decay to Heaven's fresh, new aroma of purity and life.

Jesus told the servants to bring the water pots – but He didn't use water from a nearby well. He used water DEDICATED TO PURIFICATION in pots beside the house. He used something that was set aside for God's holy purposes already. It was never "just a pot of water", but a "purification pot" set aside for God to use.

Here is the truth: God uses what we give to Him to use. What is kept for us to use as we please is not surrendered, so it doesn't get used in the marvelous display of transformation - because we don't want to give it up. Some believers aren't changing, simply because they are keeping the pots of water for themselves and not surrendering them to Jesus as He told them. They have their own religious pots, neat and clean, and their water is still just ....water. If we want transformation, we are required to surrender what we have to Jesus to get it. When they gave it to Jesus, He dramatically transformed into something outlandishly exquisite.

Don't miss the story in the water pot. God's intention for you is not that you become a raging and angry **separatist** – trying to whine your way into people's ears. What pleases Him isn't that you HATE, PROTEST and COMPLAIN. At the same time, God isn't looking for you to become a tolerant **conformist** who measures what is TRUE by what is POPULAR. God wants ONE THING that will mark your life... He wants you to deliberately yield your life choices to Him, so that He can **TRANSFORM YOUR LIFE** in front of all the people in your life. Don't worry – when he does – they won't mistake the exquisite wine for bland water. When God gets hold of a life, people smell the aroma of life and taste the spice of truth. You don't need a t-shirt, a bumper sticker or a campaign. Transformed lives are the best evangelism program any church will ever have.

While we are studying the story, let's not pass over a problem that often occurs when Jesus is at work among His followers. Don't forget that when Jesus arrived in Cana there was a problem. It seems like it was his mother's problem, or at least she *felt* responsible for some reason... What happened next is a common problem believer's will understand...she thrust HER PLAN for the problem on Jesus. It is surely true that Jesus was, at least from an earthly perspective, her son. Bu the truth is, many believers act exactly this way toward Jesus when they get into trouble. Do you see it? The text doesn't say Mary "dropped to her knees and sought God concerning the difficulty". She didn't *consult* Jesus on what should be done. MARY HAD A LITTLE PLAN and she **wanted her plan cared for by Jesus**. Can you identify with that? Did your prayer life ever sound like you were offering God sage counsel on how to fix things?

We need to be careful: We cannot tack Jesus on the plans we have already made and call that a surrendered life... it isn't. **Jesus is our Master, not our Holy errand boy**. I love that Jesus honored her request, but I don't want that to become my pattern in life.

First Challenge at Jerusalem

The story of the Cana miracle is always thrilling, because I want to be transformed and I love that God shows He can do it in dramatic ways! At the same time, the second story - the "**First Cleansing of the Temple**" (John 2:13-25) always changes the temperature in the room when I am passing through the study of John chapter two. It isn't a **happy** time, but a **serious** time of challenge.

John 2:13 The Passover of the Jews was near, and Jesus went up to Jerusalem. 14 And He found in the temple those who were selling oxen and sheep and doves, and the money changers seated [at their tables]. 15 And He made a scourge of cords, and drove [them] all out of the temple, with the sheep and the oxen; and He poured out the coins of the money changers and overturned their tables; 16 and to those who were selling the doves He said, "Take these things away; stop making My Father's house a place of business." 17 His disciples remembered that it was written, "ZEAL FOR YOUR HOUSE WILL CONSUME ME." 18 The Jews then said to Him, "What sign do You show us as your authority for doing these things?" 19 Jesus answered them, "Destroy this temple, and in three days I will raise it up." 20 The Jews then said, "It took forty-six years to build this temple, and will You raise it up in three days?" 21 But He was speaking of the temple of His body. 22 So when He was raised from the dead, His disciples remembered that He said this; and they believed the Scripture and the word which Jesus had spoken. 23 Now when He was in Jerusalem at the Passover, during the feast, many believed in His name, observing His signs which He was doing. 24 But Jesus, on His part, was not entrusting Himself to them, for He knew all men, 25 and because He did not need anyone to testify concerning man, for He Himself knew what was in man.

The time came for the feast of Pesach (Passover) and He went to Jerusalem to celebrate it. He journeyed south to Jerusalem (about 80 miles as the crow flies – cp.2:13). "Passover" was so important we have some record of authorities that would repair the roads for the great influx of people ... and whitewash the tombs so nobody would accidentally touch them and accidently defile themselves. Homes were cleaned, cooking utensils cleansed, and houses were removed of all leaven. Those living in Jerusalem were expected to put up out of town guests, so "dust bunnies" in every corner were removed. Fortunately, most homes were a simple plan and not very large.

- Jews celebrated deliverance from bondage in Egypt and Jews from all over would come to the Temple in Jerusalem to present their offerings. Animals were slaughtered, fat was burned, and blood was sprinkled on the altar. Meat was taken home, and eaten by the family in a stew. People stood in line to pay the "Temple tax" of a silver ½ shekel coin to pay for daily sacrifices through the year.

- This was the biggest event of the year. Jesus stood on to the south porch of the Temple, observing merchants selling animals and money changers hawking the crowds as the best rate providers. (2:14).

- It seems like the place sounded more like a Middle eastern open market than a place of worship and prayer, and that got under Jesus' skin because it wasn't what God wanted at all. He responded with open rebuke. (2:15).

- Some reports tell us that the High Priest's family auctioned concession stands to the various merchants and money-changers ... to the highest bidder. Merchants charged inflated prices for sacrifice animals, and inequitable rates of exchange for Temple bound coins.

When you read the account, don't get the mistaken impression that Jesus "lost it" in a heat of the moment reaction. He didn't fly off the handle. While He was walking around, observing the chaos, He carefully picked up some of the leather cords that were laying around ... used to tie up the animals that had now been sold. While He was walking, He formed into a small whip.

Stop for a second and ask what Jesus would do on the set of the televangelist that is pleading for more money for a third of their airtime. I wonder if it is not worth asking if our generation has gotten off the path that He marked for us to follow. I wonder about the many Bible belt churches that look more like social halls and town clubs than hospitals for the spiritually wounded. Someone has said: "We worship our work ... work at our play ... and play at our worship." I am not sure they are off base at all.

Jesus knew that God's plan was for His House to be a house of prayer ... a special place ... a place of worship and praise. He called it: "My Father's house" (2:16). He saw the people's attitudes and actions – just like he sees ours. Did we sing that solo to get people to notice US, or to call them to worship HIM? Did we come because we wanted to seek Jesus, or because we thought the girl we want to date might be here?

The sadness is this: Jesus saw all the decorations of worship, but not the focus of worship! He called for UNDISTRACTED worship of God. He plead for no ulterior motive – money, career, advancement, attention, affirmation...

Here is my simple question: Do we have Jesus' zeal of heart (2:17)? *Do we say, "I was glad when they said unto me, Let us go into the house of the Lord"? (cp. Psalm 69:9).*

Jesus' zeal was literally "eating Him up inside". He had a PASSION for the things of God... We are passionate about our sports ... our eating ... music...our work. Are we that passionate about worship and prayer? He did, and He wanted others to have it as well. The authorities didn't ask about the nature of His dispute, that wasn't their issue. They wanted to know: "Who do you think you are to be doing this?" (2:18).

Their objection was John's point in the narrative – that very question..."Who was Jesus anyway?" Jesus was God's Son, and He was not willing for people to PLAY AT WORSHIP and feign a surrendered life before His Father!

Why didn't they stand up to Jesus and kick Him out? There were certainly more of them than Jesus and his few disciples. That would come later in the story of the Gospel of John. For now, Jesus was operating with an authority that could be felt, and that made them hesitant! They knew this was not simply some mad man.... Emerging was a fuller picture of Who Jesus is.

He is loving, and He is tenderhearted. He is merciful and He is kind.... But that isn't all He is. He is holy. He is just... and He doesn't like people playing religious games and substituting them for a serious passion for God. When the situation called for assertive leadership He did not shrink back from the task. He didn't "let it go." HE answered with clarity and force.

Maybe a story will help:

The Chronicles of Narnia by C.S. Lewis were set in a mythical world. That world was inhabited by centaurs, dwarves, talking wolves and beavers, fawns, and all kinds of creatures more familiar to ancient Greek mythology than modern reading books. In one installment **Narnia was covered in an endless winter** as the result of a cruel White Witch – a world desperately waiting for a terribly cold winter to finally end. The central character of this book, a talking lion named Aslan (who the author said represented Christ). He was both a ruler and a Savior-type.

Four children – Lucy, Edmund, Susan, and Peter – ended up in Narnia and were educated by Mr. and Mrs. Beaver, who told them about Aslan. They learned that Aslan was the true King and the son of the "Emperor-Beyond-The-Sea." They learned that Aslan was a lion - not a man. When that truth was made plain, Susan said: "**Is he – quite safe? I shall feel rather nervous about meeting a lion**." Mr. Beaver replied, "If there's anyone who can appear before Aslan without their knees knocking, they're either braver than most or just quite silly." Then the youngest of the children, little Lucy, says, "Then he isn't safe?" Mr. Beaver replied, "Who said anything about safe? 'Course he's not safe. But he's good."

I remember that quote, because I think it says it all! Jesus is not who people think He is, and He breaks the molds we make for Him! He is not safe – He is Sovereign... and our reaction to His place in our lives determines if we really are Christians, or just religious church tourists.

Jesus knew His place, and revealed it from the very beginning of His public ministry. What He met was resistance, because people want a Rescuer, but not a Master.

Following His Footsteps:
Lesson Eight: "The Candidate" (John 3 and 4)

Robert Redford has played some famous roles, but none bigger than the Oscar winning performance in the 1972 movie called "The Candidate. In that role, Redford starred as a lawyer (and son of the former California governor) who was convinced to run against a senatorial incumbent who faced no competition. Even those who asked Redford to run anticipated a dramatic loss, so the candidate was able to run with frankness and integrity in order to demonstrate a new brand of politics. When people realized they preferred a fresh, young and honest looking face – the campaign became serious. Thirty years have passed, but the issues in that election were none other than: abortion, environmental issues, and access to health care. The Candidate demonstrated that it wasn't simply WHAT the man said, but HOW the man said it. Someone quipped: "If you can fake sincerity, you will have the world as your friend!" We are thinking about The Candidate in this lesson, because our text in John's Gospel offered some early interviews and reactions to Jesus as He began to become known.

Key Principle: Jesus brought out a reaction in people! The gospels reveal that Jesus was pressed from the beginning of His ministry by scholars, sermonizers and other sinners. He answered them all with sincerity and knowledge of their real need.

John 3 and 4 tell four stories that can easily be "paired" into sets – private interview followed by public endorsements. When you see that we are looking at two chapters of the Bible, it can seem daunting, but these four stories are actually very familiar. In addition, they follow a pattern – a private interview followed by a public story – two times. As you look deeper, you will note that in John 3, these were done in the context of mainstream Judaism, in John 4 they were in the context of a fringe group known as the Samaritans. Let's look at the stories briefly. One of the four stories we covered in a recent lesson, so we will lightly touch it:

First, there was an "interview" - a private discussion: Nicodemus the Pharisee talks with Jesus of Nazareth (John:1-21).

John 3:1 Now there was a man of the Pharisees, named Nicodemus, a ruler of the Jews; 2 this man came to Jesus by night and said to Him, "Rabbi, we know that You have come from God as a teacher; for no one can do these signs that You do unless God is with him." 3 Jesus answered and said to him, "Truly, truly, I say to you, unless one is born again he cannot see the kingdom of God." 4 Nicodemus *said to Him, "How can a man be born when he is old? He cannot enter a second time into his mother's womb and be born, can he?" 5 Jesus answered, "Truly, truly, I say to you, unless one is born of water and the Spirit he cannot enter into the kingdom of God. 6 That which is born of the flesh is flesh, and that which is born of the Spirit is spirit. 7 Do not be amazed that I said to you, 'You must be born [c]again.' 8 The wind blows where it wishes and you hear the sound of it, but do not know where it comes from and where it is going; so is everyone who is born of the Spirit." 9 Nicodemus said to Him, "How can these things be?" 10 Jesus answered and said to him, "Are you the teacher of Israel and do not understand these things? 11 Truly, truly, I say to you, we speak of what we know and testify of what we have seen, and you do not accept our testimony. 12 If I told you earthly things and you do not believe, how will you believe if I tell you heavenly things? 13 No one has ascended into heaven, but He who descended from heaven: the Son of Man. 14 As Moses lifted up the serpent in the wilderness, even so must the Son of Man be lifted up; 15 so that whoever [d]believes will in Him have eternal life. 16 "For God so loved the world, that He gave His *[e]only begotten Son, that whoever believes in Him shall not perish, but have eternal life. 17 For God did not send the Son into the world to judge the world, but that the world might be saved through Him. 18 He who believes in Him is not judged; he who does not believe has been judged already, because he has not believed in the name of the [f]only begotten Son of God. 19 This is the judgment, that the Light has come into the world, and men loved the darkness rather than the Light, for their deeds were evil. 20 For everyone who does evil hates the Light, and does not come to the Light for fear that his deeds will be exposed. 21 But he who practices the truth comes to the Light, so that his deeds may be manifested as having been wrought in God."*

The record of the conversation between Jesus and Nicodemus is the first interview of the Savior (in the Gospel of John) by a trained theologian. The exchange is offered in two parts. First, John included the context – time and people involved. Second, he included the dialogue. That exchange had three sentences offered by Nicodemus, together with the answers of the Savior, which were longer than the questions.

Look at John 3:1 closely. Don't forget the context in the story of the Gospel of John: this story of Nicodemus was set up by the penetrating truth offered at the end of John 2:25 "…He Himself knew what was in man." This story seems to be placed in the text as an illustration of Jesus reading the heart of an important man of His day. Don't overlook that John 3:1 is short, but PACKED with information that helps the rest of the exchange make sense. John recorded:

- There was a "man of the Pharisees" – this was a man of PEDIGREE of PUBLIC (if not also private) PIETY. Nicodemus held a distinguished religious position – but position doesn't make one live eternally – and this man suspected something was wrong.

- He was "named Nicodemus" a name which meant in Greek "conqueror of the people" or "the people's champion (victor)". His name suggested the intent his parents had for him was him to be popular – but popularity in the here and now does not solve the issue of afterlife.

- The next phrase remarks: "ruler of the Jews", which offered a statement of obvious POWER and PRESTIGE in the community – but power and prestige on earth doesn't translate into security for a moment after the last breath on earth.

The subject of the exchange was clearly about being "born again" – but what did that mean? Clearly this new birth was not about human accomplishment – it was something God did through the power of the Holy Spirit. Being born again was explained by Jesus as an intervention from God that leads to a TRANSFORMATION *by* God... That supernatural act was not given because of a pedigree – for no degree could get a man right with God. It was not a matter of religious reform or behavioral practice – because Nicodemus was already living righteously as best we can tell from the story. This "born again" experience was something brought from above – a transformation accomplished by the work of God.

Consider the three statements of Nicodemus that were recalled in the Gospel account. Each reflect common assumptions that still plague people and keep them from understanding salvation by Grace:

Statement One: "Externals are accurate barometers of internals". That seems to be the implied idea behind John 3:2 "This man came to Jesus by night and said to Him, "Rabbi, we know that You have come from God as a teacher; for no one can do these signs that You do unless God is with him." First, the statement is untrue. Ask Moses' brother Aaron (a story from Exodus 7) as the eighty year old Moses and eighty-three year old Aaron saw Pharaoh's black magic men make snakes just like God did. Sadly for the magicians of the court, Aaron's serpent ate all of theirs – leaving them "staff-less" in the end! The fact remains that in the Bible, JUST BECAUSE A MIRACLE TOOK PLACE, DID NOT MEAN GOD INITIATED IT.

Nicodemus assumed that the externals were accurate proof of internals.

Statement Two: "Spiritual transformation occurs because of physical activity." John 3:4 offered these words: "Nicodemus said to Him, "How can a man be born when he is old? He cannot enter a second time into his mother's womb and be born, can he?" Note how consumed the Pharisee is with the ability of the man to DO something to change the outcome of his standing with God. Here Nicodemus offered the mistaken assumption that SPIRITUAL CHANGE OCCURS BECAUSE OF PHYSICAL CHANGES ONE MAKES. In the atonement system, a man or woman's participation was NOT designed to make them think they "participated" in God's work of forgiveness, but that is the message many took away. Many who followed the Law of God ended up believing the way to change the INSIDE was to change the BEHAVIOR on the OUTSIDE. Did you ever hear a joke about people entering Heaven. They begin like: "Three men died and were standing at the pearly gates..." We have all heard these kinds of jokes and though they may bring a smile to our face, behind most of them is *the false assumption that we must do something to get into Heaven*. That wasn't the message of Jesus. The problem is that by nature, we want to *earn* and then *deserve* God's favor. That isn't the Gospel – because the message of the New Testament is that you cannot make any effective installment on the payment for sin.

Statement Three: "Only what I understand can work!" That seems to the message behind John 3:9: "Nicodemus said to Him, "How can these things be?" It would have sounded like a reasonable question in the tect, but Jesus' answer showed that it was nothing of the sort. Nicodemus was assuming that in order for things to be true, they had to fit into his considerable knowledge of the spiritual world – and that wasn't true at all. His assumption seemed to be, IF IT DOESN'T FIT MY UNDERSTANDING, IT MUST BE NONSENSE! Jesus poured it on at the end with a rather detailed reply to his question.

Jesus each question Nicodemus offered...

Answer One: "Total transformation is needed, and that isn't from the outside." In John 3:3 we read Jesus' response to the idea that externals are reliable barometers of internals: "Jesus answered and said to him, "Truly, truly, I say to you, unless one is born again he cannot see the kingdom of God." The Savior offered words that set Nicodemus back on his heels – that one can ONLY see the kingdom if they are **REBORN**. Technically speaking, a baby doesn't CAUSE their birth – and though the pass through the birth canal – no one observing closely in the birthing suite at the hospital would think they were in charge of the event. A man or woman needed to START LIFE AGAIN – this time as a newborn all over again. The point of the statement that "only by being born again" is this: Nicodemus, you must totally rethink your premise. Entering the Kingdom is NOT by conforming to a set of rules, reforming your lifestyle to a certain set of rules… it is being transformed by a process YOU DO NOT CONTROL!

Answer Two: "The new birth is a spiritual reality, but no less real than physical birth." In John 3:5 Jesus answered, "Truly, truly, I say to you, unless one is born of water and the Spirit he cannot enter into the kingdom of God. 6 "That which is born of the flesh is flesh, and that which is born of the Spirit is spirit. 7 "Do not be amazed that I said to you, 'You must be born again.' 8 "The wind blows where it wishes and you hear the sound of it, but do not know where it comes from and where it is going; so is everyone who is born of the Spirit."

This was a three point response:

First, two types of birth are necessary to be in the kingdom – a physical birth and a spiritual birth. You are not born spiritually WHEN you are born physically. There is no special class of "child of believer" that exempts them from the later spiritual new birth experience. No one is physically born right with God.

Second, the two births are distinct from one another. The spiritual birth is LIKE the physical, but not the same thing.

Third, those born of the spirit are compared to the wind – the **effects** of wind can be seen without the **work** of the wind being displayed. It is the nature of religious people to look for ways to observe God's hand. Ironically, whole church movements that began with an emphasis on the work of the Spirit have found themselves tilting quickly into a theology that emphasizes blessing in the physical world... even though Jesus said they were not reliably connected – at least in appearance.

Answer Three: "God will not negotiate this requirement!" In John 3:10 "Jesus answered and said to him, "Are you the teacher of Israel and do not understand these things? ... 16 "For God so loved the world, that He gave His only begotten Son, that whoever believes in Him shall not perish, but have eternal life. 17 "For God did not send the Son into the world to judge the world, but that the world might be saved through Him. 18 "He who believes in Him is not judged; he who does not believe has been judged already, because he has not believed in the name of the only begotten Son of God."

The answer Jesus offered was this: First, a true teacher of God's people should understand transformation by the Spirit is required! Second, this was not a theory, nor an option (3:11). Third, failure to grab the transformation blocks other truth from your heart (3:12). Fourth, Jesus was the only source of this transformation (3:13). Fifth, failure to get behind this message will block your ability to lead others to eternal life (3:14-15). Sixth, Jesus came to SAVE men (3:16-17). His message was God's MERCY AND GRACE. Seventh, the sole basis of judgment is belief in Jesus' Word. People could choose not to believe and live in the darkness of their own controls! (3:18-21).

Here is the truth: Jesus wanted a learned man to come away from the interview with one clear message: "You need a total transformation that I control." That reminds me of the old story of someone who asked revivalist preacher George Whitfield, "Why do you always preach "You must be born again?" He replied, "Because you must be born again!" The interview completed, the message was clear – Jesus didn't come to offer us a list of reforms – He came to offer new birth, a total transformation of a life submitted to His care.

Second, there was a public endorsement: John the Baptizer commended Jesus (John 3:22-35).

Since we looked at this passage a few lessons ago, we need not give it much more time and space – but stop briefly and consider how John's reaction to Jesus' ministry affected Jesus...

The Gospel writer recorded: John 3:22 "After these things Jesus and His disciples came into the land of Judea, and there He was spending time with them and baptizing. 23 John also was baptizing in Aenon near Salim, because there was much water there; and people were coming and were being baptized ... 27 John ... said... 30 "He must increase, but I must decrease. 31 "He who comes from above is above all, he who is of the earth is from the earth and speaks of the earth. He who comes from heaven is above all. ... 36 He who believes in the Son has eternal life; but he who does not obey the Son will not see life, but the wrath of God abides on him."

John recognized Who Jesus was, and was unafraid to endorse Him publicly – in spite of the fact that people may decide to stop showing up at the Jordan to see John and his disciples. John's logic: "It doesn't matter – He is above all and before all." Let's say it in simpler terms that any believer can learn to respect: "Jesus first!" The truth is that Scripture records that John laid down his life long before his head was placed on a platter or his neck on a chopping block. He laid his life down when he decided that Jesus' glory was worth living for – and that is inherently Christian teaching. A theology of personal abandonment and Christocentric glory is the very essence of the first century disciple's life choices. Jesus was clear to those who wished to get on board with His gang: "Unless they were willing to take up their cross daily, laying their lives down – they could not become His disciple.

Here's the truth: Jesus isn't willing to share the stage with His followers. Either we get the fact that He is Lord and we are His servant – or we don't recognize the paradigm of discipleship that Jesus offered. A Christian message that is oriented to offering us temporal benefits – a happier life, better relationships, more money in the bank, a better job – all these are not specifically Christian at all. Ask the believers who just fled from Mosul if knowing and loving Jesus guaranteed a happy life and peaceful experience? We have to stop repeating nonsense and get back to Christian teaching the way Jesus framed it. HE is what we get from surrender. Where HE leads is what will bring HIM glory. My best good is found in HIS plan for HIS pleasure. Christianity cannot be about self-aggrandizing and self-affirmation or it isn't Christianity at all. John understood – and John laid down his life. Jesus said that is the kind of man who will LIVE because he died to self.

Third, there was another private interview: The Samaritan woman at the well met Jesus (John 4:1-29).

A third story can be found in the beginning of John 4, and we again find ourselves looking at a personal interview – this time with a Samaritan woman. How different than a Pharisee! She was wounded by life and covered the wounds with theological discourse. On second thought: "Was she actually that much different than Nicodemus?" Here is the record:

John 4:3 He [Jesus] left Judea and went away again into Galilee. 4 And He had to pass through Samaria. 5 So He came to a city of Samaria called Sychar, ... 7 There *came a woman of Samaria to draw water. Jesus said to her, "Give Me a drink." 8 For His disciples had gone away into the city to buy food. 9 Therefore the Samaritan woman said to Him, "How is it that You, being a Jew, ask me for a drink since I am a Samaritan woman?" (For Jews have no dealings with Samaritans.) 10 Jesus answered and said to her, "If you knew the gift of God, and who it is who says to you, 'Give Me a drink,' you would have asked Him, and He would have given you living water." 11 She *said to Him, "[b]Sir, You have nothing to draw with and the well is deep; where then do You get that living water? 12 You are not greater than our father Jacob, are You, who gave us the *well, and drank of it himself and his sons and his cattle?" 13 Jesus answered and said to her, "Everyone who drinks of this water will thirst again; 14 but whoever drinks of the water that I will give him shall never thirst; but the water that I will give him will become in him a well of water springing up to eternal life." 15 The woman *said to Him, "[c]Sir, give me this water, so I will not be thirsty nor come all the way here to draw." 16 He *said to her, "Go, call your husband and come here." 17 The woman answered and said, "I have no husband." Jesus *said to her, "You have correctly said, 'I have no husband'; 18 for you have had five husbands, and the one whom you now have is not your husband; this you have said truly." 19 The woman *said to Him, "[d]Sir, I perceive that You are a prophet. 20 Our fathers worshiped in this mountain, and you people say that in Jerusalem is the place where men ought to worship." 21 Jesus *said to her, "Woman, believe Me, an hour is coming when neither in this mountain nor in Jerusalem will you worship the Father. 22 You worship what you do not know; we worship what we know, for salvation is from the Jews. 23 But an hour is coming, and now is, when the true worshipers will worship the Father in spirit and truth; for such people the Father seeks to be His worshipers. 24 God is [e]spirit, and those who worship Him must worship in spirit and truth." 25 The woman *said to Him, "I know that Messiah is coming (He who is called Christ); when that One comes, He will declare all things to us." 26 Jesus *said to her, "I who speak to you am He." ...28 So the woman left her waterpot, and went into the city and *said to the men, 29 "Come, see a man who told me all the things that I have done; this is not the Christ, is it?...."*

It is easy to divide the story into three parts, as John recalls the events: First, the Setting (4:1-6), second, the Exchange (4:7-28), and finally the Results (4:29-42).

The interview lasted for only a short time, but the woman appeared to move from broken to hopeful. How did that happen? Look again. The woman spoke six times in the passage – five of them to Jesus. In the five direct statements, there was a progression to her thinking. Often, when people are confronted with the direction that Jesus offers, they place "road blocks" - objections to the uncomfortable truth - yet Jesus knew how to deal with her objections.

Let me offer a simple observation. Nicodemus was an example that no one can become so great as to **rise above** the need for the Savior. Yet, the Samaritan woman (a page later in the story) was a great example that no one can **sink below** the rescue of the Savior, either!

The Samaritan woman raised some common objections to Jesus and His message:

First, there was a doubt of intention: What does Jesus *really* want from me? (4:9) Clearly the woman was stunned that Jesus as a Jew would ask her as a Samaritan for something to drink. Yet, on more careful examination, it appears that she was not only asking why a Jew would speak to her, but she was exposing a very basic reaction that many people have when Jesus reaches out to them. The Gospel offers life, but it also requires something of them. Without submission of the will there is no real salvation. Jesus began ASKING FOR HER TO DO SOMETHING FOR HIM. The simple act of giving a drink to Jesus was an act of obedience – an act of trust.

Second, there was a sense of unworthiness: How can you deal with someone LIKE ME? Many people carry the misconception Jesus came for, and spent His time with religious people in clean and tidy places. That is not the Jesus of the Gospels. This woman knew prejudice and rejection – and she wasn't living with someone who valued her highly – which is why she came midday alone to get water! Jesus' answer was direct to her – You are worried about who you are and what I may really want. Both are the wrong focus. If you refocus on Who I am, you will find a gift is awaiting you! (4:10). Yet, in order for her to receive the gift, she needed to THIRST TO KNOW HIM!

Third, there was doubt of His ability: Jesus made an overt claim that He had something to GIVE the woman, but she couldn't see how it was possible for Jesus to deliver on the promises (4:11). She chided, "You don't think you are greater than our fathers, do you? (4:12). Wrapped in her question is one of the oldest forms of objection to Jesus and His message. She wanted to compare Jesus to other great men, and didn't see how He could claim to offer more than other men of seemingly greater stature could offer. Jesus' answer was again direct and overt – I am not one among many. That is the wrong conclusion. Jesus said, in essence: "I have the gift and the ability to deliver it." (4:13-14). It will surely accomplish satisfaction beginning within and flowing outward. It is superior to anything offered before, and it will deliver the ultimate and final rewards.

Fourth, there was a distraction over benefits: The woman appeared to be ready to accept the offer made by Jesus, but Jesus knew she was not truly prepared. There was a hole in her heart, and He wanted to address it. She was distracted by the part of the offer that appeared to care for her problems, but she did not comprehend what Jesus wanted from her (4:15). Jesus peeled into her life to help her expose the deep secret that she was hiding. He asked her to go and bring her husband. This was a respectful request, especially if she was about to make a bold move to accept His claims and follow Jesus (4:16). The woman replied, "I have no husband!" She told a half-truth (4:17-18). She was a woman who both lived in pain, and as a result walked in hidden compromise. Here is the central issue – she wanted to add Jesus to a life of self-will and hidden impure behaviors. That is a wrong assumption. It is true that Jesus loves us. It is true that He came to save us. It is simply NOT TRUE that He is so longing for us that He will simply dismiss our desire to continue to walk as we choose – in sinful practices that are forbidden by God. Hidden sin robs us of full joy – and Jesus wanted her change to be honest.

Because we know that in the first century Jewish context, divorce was an issue of a man putting away a woman in most cases – it is likely that the woman's history of marriages has more to do with stinging repeated rejection and not simply a life as a "loose woman". She was evidently repeatedly judged deficient in some way by the men in her life. Rejection upon rejection appears to have left her desolate of self respect. She eventually shed the need to even have the appearance of a real marriage (4:18).

Charles Swindoll, in his book Growing Deep in the Christian Life, tells the true story of a man who bought fried chicken dinners for himself and his girlfriend to enjoy on a picnic one afternoon. He was in for a surprise because the person behind the counter mistakenly gave him the wrong paper bag. Earlier, the manager had taken the money from the cash registers and placed it in an ordinary bag, hoping to disguise it on his way to the bank. But when the person working the cash register went to give the man his order, he grabbed the bag full of money instead of the bag full of chicken. Swindoll says, "After driving to their picnic site, the two of them sat down to enjoy some chicken. They discovered a whole lot more than chicken — over $800! But he was unusual. He quickly put the money back in the bag. They got back into the car and drove all the way back. Mr. Clean got out, walked in, and became an instant hero. By then, the manager was frantic. The guy with the bag of money looked the manager in the eye and said, 'I want you to know I came by to get a couple of chicken dinners and wound up with all this money here.' Well, the manager was thrilled to death. He said, 'Let me call the newspaper. I'm gonna have your picture put in the local paper. You're one of the most honest men I've ever heard of.' To which the man quickly responded, 'Oh, no. No, no, don't do that!' Then he leaned closer and whispered, 'You see, the woman I'm with is not my wife. She's, uh, somebody else's wife.'" Swindoll closes the story by saying, "Harder to find than lost cash is a perfect heart."

Fifth, there was theological redirection: Jesus spoke resounding truth into the life of the woman, and she knew it. He opened her eyes to the truth about her own pain and made clear that He knew all about it. He peeled her heart to its core. She perceived He was a prophet. Yet, she was not ready to surrender to Jesus. She re-directed the conversation to theology and arguments over the place and nature of worship, emphasizing the difference between Jews and Samaritans (4:19-20). Jesus answered her and told her that she was essentially on the wrong issue. She was concerned with the PLACE of worship, and Jesus answered with the NATURE of worship (4:21-24). Getting caught up in any discussion that kept away the pressure on the woman to yield her broken heart to the Lord, no matter the value of the discussion, was a distraction.

Sixth, there was the voice of procrastination: "Someday I hope it will happen for me!" was the final objection raised (4:25). *Many* have raised it. "One of these days, when things work out for me, then I will be ready to commit to Jesus." Jesus replied to the woman, "You are on the wrong timing!" The time for her salvation was the day Jesus beckoned. Later would be too late.

Fourth, there was another public endorsement: The Samaritan Union validated the ministry of Jesus (John 4:39ff).

Before we finish with our lesson, one more short story is necessary to review – the reaction of the Samaritans to the woman's testimony. John recorded:

John 4:39 From that city many of the Samaritans believed in Him because of the word of the woman who testified, "He told me all the things that I have done." 40 So when the Samaritans came to Jesus, they were asking Him to stay with them; and He stayed there two days. ... 43 After the two days He went forth from there into Galilee..."

Jesus chatted with one woman and the message of His life and ministry reached a village. The disciples went as a group to shop in the midst of the village and reached NO ONE. Why? The answer lies in the truth that Jesus did what they did not want to do. In order to bring about healing to the lives of others, we must first learn to become lovers of the unlovable...that is what our Savior did.

Years ago, in a moving short story by Elizabeth Ballard that was published in Home Life magazine (1976) the fine fiction writer wove a touching story that really helps set love in perspective.

Who the story was based on in her life we shall never know. Here is the story:

Teddy Stallard was a young man who was turned off by school. He was sloppy in appearance, largely expressionless in class, and generally unattractive. Some would have called him "slow" – because he had a "dull look". Often he sat in his school classroom staring into space, unresponsive and blank - which was an irritation to every teacher he ever had. Miss Thompson, who was known to have enjoyed bearing down her red pen -- placed many a big red X beside Teddy's often blank and mostly wrong answers. If only she had studied Ted's school records more carefully. They read:

- 1st grade: Ted shows promise with his work and attitude, but (has) poor home situation.
- 2nd grade: Ted could do better. Mother seriously ill. Receives little help from home.
- 3rd grade: Ted is good boy but too serious. He is a slow learner. His mother died this year.
- 4th grade: Ted is very slow, but well-behaved. His father shows no interest whatsoever.

Christmas arrived. The children piled elaborately wrapped gifts on their teacher's desk. Ted brought one too. It was wrapped in brown paper and held together with Scotch Tape. Miss Thompson opened each gift, as the children crowded around to watch. Out of Ted's package fell a gaudy rhinestone bracelet, with half of the stones missing along with a bottle of cheap perfume. The children snickered, but the wise teacher silenced them by splashing some of the perfume on her wrist and letting them smell it. She put the bracelet on too. At day's end, after the other children left, Ted came by the teacher's desk and said, "Miss Thompson, you smell just like my mother. And the bracelet looks real pretty on you. I'm glad you like my presents." He left. Miss Thompson got down on her knees and asked God to forgive her and to change her attitude. The next day, the children were greeted by a reformed teacher -- one committed to loving each of them...especially the slower and harder to love ones...especially Teddy.

Surprisingly -- or perhaps not surprisingly at all, Teddy began to improve in class. He eventually caught up with most of the students and excelled beyond a few. Graduation came and went and Teddy was gone into the world. Miss Thompson heard nothing from him for a long time. Then, one day, she received a note: Dear Miss Thompson: I wanted you to be the first to know. I will be graduating second in my class. Love, Ted

Four years later, another note arrived: Dear Miss Thompson: They just told me I will be graduating first in my class. I wanted you to be first to know. The university has not been easy, but I liked it. Love, Ted

And four years later:

Dear Miss Thompson: As of today, I am Theodore Stallard, M.D. How about that? I wanted you to be the first to know. I am getting married next month, the 27th to be exact. I want you to come and sit where my mother would sit if she were alive. You are the only family I have now; Dad died last year. Love, Ted

Miss Thompson attended that wedding, and sat where Ted's mother would have sat. The compassion she had shown that young man entitled her to that privilege.

I love that story, and I am glad that Elizabeth Ballard wrote it. It isn't bad to have our hearts tugged to learn an important lesson. Here is the truth: Jesus brought out a reaction in people! He was pressed from the beginning of His ministry by scholars, sermonizers and other sinners – but He knew the hearts of people – so He knew how to respond…and He still does.

Following His Footsteps:
Lesson Nine: "Rising Star" (Mt. 4:17; Mk. 1:14b-15; John 4:46-54)

"The hardest part was at the very beginning!" said the young pop music star. "I came along before there was an 'American Idol' show, but just *after* the big record labels were already losing to the digital market of iTunes and Napster. That window was very hard to get started in this business!" the young woman complained. Truthfully, I didn't know who she was, but her interview caught my attention on the TV set above my head. Of course, the fact that my flight was going to be delayed and my sandwich was utterly uninteresting may have also had something to do with my interest in her interview. I watched the whole exchange and then my mind drifted. Getting started... sometimes that really IS the hardest part. My mind faded back to my home:

...My hedges need clipping, but to do it I'd have to get the clippers and the cord out and drag them through the hot backyard in the Florida summer sun... I think that can wait!

...I really need to start this diet and drop off these extra summer pounds that came from writing for hours in a chair, but to do that I have to get the stuff to make those morning breakfast shakes in the cupboard, and besides... there is a pan of brownies in the kitchen that shouldn't go to waste...

...I need to paint the woodwork upstairs, but in order to do that I will need to check in the garage on the pan and brushes, and that garage is a mess. I am not sure where the paint is, and that is going to be another fiasco to get the right color...

Anyone who wrestles with themselves to get things done knows that **starting** isn't easy. It takes commitment, and you have to believe that it is both important and able to be accomplished. Today's lesson is about the beginnings of the public ministry of Jesus – the "getting started" in crowd teaching, healing and shepherding. Jesus was stepping out of the shadows into center stage in some Galilee villages. After Nicodemus was taught by

Jesus to see life in a new way, and the Samaritan "woman at the well" in Sychar found that her life was not empty and useless – Jesus made His way back to the western lower Galilee, to the region where He had grown up years before. **The first interviews were concluded**, and Jesus was now working with growing crowds and a handful of disciples that John sent his way. Jesus needed to make His message known, and back it up with significant works to show His power. Four short passages recall this time of ministry, and each offers a view that includes different **problems** and different **reasons to believe** in Jesus and His message.

Key Principle: Though some ignore the Savior's true message in favor a religious control or a self-directed life, those who trust Jesus find Him to be the answer God promised long before His coming.

The short passages found in both Matthew's Gospel and that of the Gospel of Mark tell us the same thing about the beginning of Jesus' public ministry – it began with public preaching. Jesus was not simply some philanthropist – He was a public preacher.

Preaching: It is time for repentance and Kingdom preparation (Mt. 4:17; Mk. 1:14b-15).

Note the two records and what they offer us about the message of the Savior at the outset:

Mt. 4:17 "From that time Jesus began to preach and say, "Repent, for the kingdom of heaven is at hand."

Mk. 1:14 "...Jesus came into Galilee, preaching the gospel of God, 15 and saying, "The time is fulfilled, and the kingdom of God is at hand; repent and believe in the gospel."

First, Jesus' preaching was, from its beginning, about BEHAVIOR, not simply about Pharisaism or "world peace." That is a more important point than we may have believed in time past, because people in our country have been consistently told otherwise. Listen to the words of the text – Jesus said four things if the two accounts are taken together:

The time had come: God has a plan, and He unspooled events to coincide with His purposes. God chose a time when a portion of Judah had been returned to the ancient homeland of Israel. He chose to send Jesus into a time when a singular language gripped much of the western world. He offered His Son when the Roman Empire – a politically contrived power – was blending many languages, cultures and cultic worship forms into one cohesive unit around the Mediterranean. He picked a moment in the timeline of human history that He knew would work the best for His plan.

Repentance was necessary: Meeting God is always on His terms. Jesus didn't tell people to "fix themselves", but rather to turn away from their self-determined path and follow Him. That "turnabout" is the meaning of the word "repent" (meta-noeo). The implication is that change must come. As long as one believes they can apprehend God by their own seeking, the need for a Savior is tiny. If one doesn't see themselves as "lost" they seek no Savior. The requirement of repentance was this: Know you have a need and that you cannot find it within, or in any religious system you currently possess.

The Kingdom was near: Where the King goes, the kingdom follows. The Jesus of the New Testament was the "Eternal Son of God" involved as the very agent of Creation (Colossians 1:16-17). He is the "expressed image of God's person" (Hebrews 1). Because He was the promised King that would one day sit on the throne of David, the Kingdom was near. It would be enacted, first spiritually and later physically… but God always delivers His promises.

It was time to believe in the Good News: The coming of the "Perfect Lamb" that John the Baptizer made clear "came to take away the sin of the world" was very good news. The system of atonement was never-ending with death and bloodshed – a graphic reminder of sin and the payment in blood and death. The message that Jesus' sacrifice, as gruesome and horrible as it was made, was the total payment was very good news. Sheep and goats applauded along with their human owners! His death was their life – and that was good news.

As long as people believe they can earn God's forgiveness through religious or philanthropic deeds, they will maintain their own control over their spiritual destiny, and therein is the lie. God has a plan, and God provided the Lamb when it suited Him to do so. The message came with the King – the Kingdom was coming next.

Power: Healing long distance (John 4:46-54).

During the early days of His preaching, Jesus returned to Cana (sometime after He had turned water into wine at a wedding). People were excited to have Him back, and I am sure He had **plenty of invitations** for upcoming parties! John's Gospel recorded:

John 4:46 Therefore He came again to Cana of Galilee where He had made the water wine. And there was a royal official whose son was sick at Capernaum. 47 When he heard that Jesus had come out of Judea into Galilee, he went to Him and was imploring Him to come down and heal his son; for he was at the point of death. 48 So Jesus said to him, "Unless you people see signs and wonders, you simply will not believe." 49 The royal official said to Him, "Sir, come down before my child dies." 50 Jesus said to him, "Go; your son lives." The man believed the word that Jesus spoke to him and started off. 51 As he was now going down, his slaves met him, saying that his son was living. 52 So he inquired of them the hour when he began to get better. Then they said to him, "Yesterday at the seventh hour the fever left him." 53 So the father knew that it was at that hour in which Jesus said to him, "Your son lives "; and he himself believed and his whole household. 54 This is again a second sign that Jesus performed when He had come out of Judea into Galilee.

By including this short episode, John offered us the opportunity to observe the happenings in Cana, and recorded a story that can easily be broken into three simple parts:

- **The Encounter with Jesus** (4:46-50a): the official left Capernaum and traveled up the steep climbing road to Cana. He met Jesus and explained his need, and Jesus obliged and told him the child was healed.

- **The Trust in Jesus** (4:50b-52): the second half of verse fifty began with the simple statement that "the man believed". The truth of that belief was illustrated in his journey home.

- **The Full Grasp of Belief** (4:53-54): as the healing of his son was made plain, the man knew how to connect his son's change to Jesus' words.

Let's move into the verses and examine the "encounter with Jesus" (4:46-50a). Though the man was a "royal official", he was also a father. This desperate dad heard of the reputation of Jesus and sought out a rescuer for his child. We know three things about the man. First, the man knew of Jesus and what others claimed He could do (4:46a). Second, the man was faced with a heart rending problem he could not care for (4:46b). Third, the man reached out for Jesus and begged Him to have mercy and deliver him from the clutches of the terrible need (4:47).

The troubles of his son led the man to abandon any sense his self-sufficiency and seek Jesus. He was an official, but he was unwilling to mask his vulnerability. In a way, his son's plight became the source of a great blessing from God, but it was found only when desperation opened his heart and made him willing to take his need to Jesus, abandoning self-reliance. The man had to traverse both the steep upward path from Capernaum to Cana and the humility of the social difference in status between Jesus and himself. Under normal circumstances this reach "downward" would have been unthinkable. This nobleman had to "lower himself" to seek help from a humble Jewish villager and now roaming preacher.

It is worth remembering that when we speak to people who are "at the top of their game" that there is no home into which pain, sickness and sorrow cannot enter. The most accomplished athlete, the most popular celebrity – every person lives within fragile bodies and in a fallen world. Our power, glory and strength can be reduced in the turn of a single news cycle of events. With the wrong word, we can watch our popularity recede faster than our hairline. When a person speaks in arrogance, it is often because they are not yet far enough along the journey – but their day will come. Troubles and pains, sickness and death – these realities humble every man or woman who isn't senseless. It is for that reason we should look beyond arrogance and anger, and see a person within.

Jesus met the official, and listened to his need (4:47) but His initial response did not seem helpful. Jesus said that Galileans only seemed to believe what they could SEE. (4:48). Is that strange? Jesus' reaction did not sound loving at all – is seemed cold. He said (apparently to the crowd around Him): "Unless you people see miraculous signs and wonders you will never believe." Why take a seemingly desperate man and hold out on him like that? The answer is not as complicated as it may appear. Remember, this is another story in the string of John's narrative, like Nicodemus and the Samaritan woman – and each illustrate an earlier statement of that Gospel: "Jesus knew the heart of man" (John 2:24-25). Jesus knew how manipulative people can be – especially those who have been in positions of power. Most of us can readily admit that we will move heaven and earth to achieve what we want. When the miracle is something as pure as healing for a child or when the miracle or God intervention is something else. The sad truth is, though, when it's done we will show no commitment to Him or His message – but will move through life in our own plan and strength. Many of us need to admit we use God to get what we want rather than allow the struggle to lead us to full submission to God.

God has an objective in the troubles of our lives – but it may surprise us. His objective is our trust in Him in all times and circumstances. People say: "If God is a healer, then why are there sick children in the world? If God is peaceful, then why do wars happen? If God loves, then why do bad things happen to good people?" Behind these questions there is the desire to see God prove himself by taking these evil things away so that we will all believe in Him and live 'happily ever after.' The problem is reframed and God's goodness is questioned - not our submission to Him based on what He has already done. In this scenario, God left Himself cloaked and refused to do what was necessary to make us believe. Our disbelief then, is HIS FAULT... but the problem is framed over false logic. Think about it: There are plenty who have enough to eat, aren't struggling with the effects of war, a roof over their heads. Yet many of those people have no relationship with God. There have been many good times in our lives that did not yield surrendered lives. Our relationship with God cannot be simply based on his ability to heal us or perform other miracles for us. Our faith must leave this world's way of thinking and take on a Biblical world view, solely based on surrender to the Word of Jesus.

Why didn't Jesus make it easy for the man? In our modern American lifestyle, we often act as though life should be easy. Ease, in fact is not always what is best for us. A faith that requires no effort is a faith that is not worth having. Faith takes effort because it requires a change on our part. It comes from God, Ephesians tells us – and not from within us. A new king sits upon the throne only after a pitted struggle removed the former king!

Jesus told the man that he could trust the Word alone – "Your son is made well." (4:50a). What is clear on close inspection is that the man changed when he encountered Jesus. Panic fled away. The 'need to trust only what he could see' left him... as he exchanged panic for trust (4:50b). How do I know? Let's take a closer look...Jesus spoke to the man at one o'clock (the seventh hour of the daylight - 4:52b) and yet did not return the same day. The text is clear the man encountered his slaves "the next day". How could this be? He came with panic in his heart and yet stayed from one o'clock in the afternoon until the next day to journey down the five and one half hour path to his home? The key to the change is the word "BELIEVED" in verse 50.

The man *believed*. The man *trusted* the word of Jesus. He rested in the promise of Jesus overnight. He "ceased striving" to find a way to care for the need because he believed the need was already met.

Sometimes, it even takes time to find out if the surrender is real: A young woman had become critically ill and her prognosis was grim; she would likely die within the year. Her family had a nominal "Easter and Christmas" commitment to the church, so the discussions in the hospital between this young pastor and the family always ploughed new ground. The woman challenged him – if Jesus healed in the Bible, He should be able to heal me today. If not, what use was He? So she begged and bargained. "If only" God would show mercy, the family urged, they would completely recommit themselves... This earnest young pastor prayed with all his heart. He refused to join the ranks of those who said, "If it is thy will." It was God's will that she be healed, he concluded. Then to his amazement, God healed her— completely. And with the physicians shaking their heads, she was sent home from the hospital. Next Sunday, the entire family was there in the front pew, dressed and sparkling. The young woman gave her testimony, praising God for his goodness. The following Sunday, the family was there again. In four weeks, it was only the woman and her husband. And after that, attendance was sporadic until they dropped into their previous pattern. Before long, the woman rationalized the entire incident. She had experienced the most dramatic sign God could give her: healing, bathed in prayer and surrounded by the church. But after only two months, its power dimmed to nothing. (Adapted from Source: sermon central illustrations).

Her surrender was not real, though her amazement was. She was amazed at first that God could and would act on her behalf. If our encounter is with amazement alone, it will fade. If our encounter led us to true surrender – we will ever be changed and marked by our walk with Jesus. Jesus is looking for surrender to Him, not an applause line from an amazed admirer. In the royal official, He got a surrendered heart.

Problems: Facing hometown rejection (Luke 4:16-31a).

*Luke 4:16 And He came to Nazareth, where He had been brought up; and as was His custom, He entered the synagogue on the Sabbath, and stood up to read. 17 And the book of the prophet Isaiah was handed to Him. And He opened the book and found the place where it was written, 18 "THE SPIRIT OF THE LORD IS UPON ME, BECAUSE HE ANOINTED ME TO PREACH THE GOSPEL TO THE POOR. HE HAS SENT ME TO PROCLAIM RELEASE TO THE CAPTIVES, AND RECOVERY OF SIGHT TO THE BLIND, TO SET FREE THOSE WHO ARE OPPRESSED, 19 TO PROCLAIM THE FAVORABLE YEAR OF THE LORD." 20 And He closed the book, gave it back to the attendant and sat down; and the eyes of all in the synagogue were fixed on Him. 21 And He began to say to them, "**Today this Scripture has been fulfilled in your hearing**." 22 And all were speaking well of Him, and wondering at the gracious words which were falling from His lips; and they were saying, "Is this not Joseph's son?" 23 And He said to them, "No doubt you will quote this proverb to Me, 'Physician, heal yourself! **Whatever we heard was done at Capernaum, do here in your hometown as well**.' " 24 And He said, "Truly I say to you, **no prophet is welcome in his hometown**. 25 "But I say to you in truth, there were many widows in Israel in the days of Elijah, when the sky was shut up for three years and six months, when a great famine came over all the land; 26 and yet Elijah was sent to none of them, but only to Zarephath, in the land of Sidon, to a woman who was a widow. 27 "And there were many lepers in Israel in the time of Elisha the prophet; and none of them was cleansed, but only Naaman the Syrian." 28 And all the people in the synagogue were filled with rage as they heard these things; 29 and they got up and drove Him out of the city, and led Him to the brow of the hill on which their city had been built, in order to throw Him down the cliff. 30 But passing through their midst, He* *went His way. 31 And He came down to Capernaum, a city of Galilee, and He was teaching them on the Sabbath;*

Four observations struck me in this story:

First, it is interesting that the **Holy Spirit led Jesus to conflict** (Matthew 4:1-13) and **ONLY THEN to fame**, when the temptation to fulfill a mission for self-motivation had been clearly defeated. (Matthew 4:14). Jesus was not taken off His mission or message by the affirmation of the crowds, but He understood the need to remain on message regardless of the response (4:22-24).

Second, **Jesus established a reputation of teaching that caused others to take him seriously** (4:15), but only **after they had observed His life** (cp. 2:52). His life was marked by the commitment to worship and the Word (4:16).

Third, Jesus' understanding of both His mission and of the crowds was bathed in His **knowledge of the Word**, and the examples of Elijah (cp. 1 Kings 17:9ff) and Elisha (2 Kings 5:1-14; 4:25-28). He framed the situation and the response to it from Biblical examples – because that was the source of truth.

Fourth, Jesus **responded to opposition with strength and surety** (4:29-30) neither harming the opposition, nor acquiescing to them. It is not necessary to "win" a discussion that uncovers people in conflict with God (or even the notion that He exists). You must strive only to be **clear** and **not be derailed**. We should concentrate on speaking Biblical truth with grace and show patient love toward the dissenting voice. It isn't our job to **make** people believe in God or the goodness of His plan, but to show how belief works out in the practice of our life. Their heart is ultimately their responsibility.

Prophecy: Settling down by the Kinnereth (Mt. 4:13-17).

There is yet one more short passage that captured the landscape of the start of Jesus' preaching, and it is found in Matthew 4:

Matthew 4:12 Now when Jesus heard that John had been taken into custody, He withdrew into Galilee; 13 and leaving Nazareth, He came and settled in Capernaum, which is by the sea, in the region of Zebulun and Naphtali. 14 This was to fulfill what was spoken through Isaiah the prophet: 15 "THE LAND OF ZEBULUN AND THE LAND OF NAPHTALI, BY THE WAY OF THE SEA, BEYOND THE JORDAN, GALILEE OF THE GENTILES - 16 "THE PEOPLE WHO WERE SITTING IN DARKNESS SAW A GREAT LIGHT, AND THOSE WHO WERE SITTING IN THE LAND AND SHADOW OF DEATH, UPON THEM A LIGHT DAWNED." 17 From that time Jesus began to preach and say, "Repent, for the kingdom of heaven is at hand."

The summary statement in verse seventeen was at the heart of the first part of this lesson – that Jesus came "out of the gate" with a message of repentance. Our second story reminded us that submission was a non-negotiable point in Jesus' work. His time in Nazareth illustrated that Jesus was undeterred in His presentation – He would not be led by family or follower – but by His Father and the mission given to Him from above. This last portion reminds us that the mission was not a new innovation, but a long expressed prophecy. Jesus was following a path that was revealed to prophets long before His birth in Bethlehem.

What appeared to be a REJECTION in Nazareth was a signal to move to Capernaum near the Kinnereth (Sea of Galilee). Matthew 4:14 made clear this was NOT a simple choice – but the fulfillment of a designed work that was already stated. Think about that for a moment. God made a plan, and even the choice to move "home base" was a part of that plan.

Was not the arrest of Jesus part of that plan? How about the striking of the face of the Savior by wicked men? Was the Cross itself part of that plan? Listen to words about the Savior written seven hundred years before His birth:

Isaiah 53:3 "He was despised and forsaken of men, A man of sorrows and acquainted with grief; And like one from whom men hide their face He was despised, and we did not esteem Him. 4 Surely our griefs He Himself bore, And our sorrows He carried; Yet we ourselves esteemed Him stricken, Smitten of God, and afflicted. 5 But He was pierced through for our transgressions, He was crushed for our iniquities; The chastening for our well-being fell upon Him, And by His scourging we are healed. 6 All of us like sheep have gone astray, Each of us has turned to his own way; But the LORD has caused the iniquity of us all To fall on Him."

Here is the point: What looked like a spontaneous rejection of his neighbors was part of a bigger plan. What appeared to be a failure to reach people with a message of love was also part of that plan. Jesus' life was pre-scripted and pre-revealed in prophetic narratives. His earth ministry wasn't about self-choice, but about following His Father's plan... and so is yours. You have few plans to make... you have paths to follow. You do not know what they are – so you must trust the One who does.

There is an old story about a potato farmer who had a son. The farmer was old, but the son young and strong. The son was accused of theft and thrown in jail – and the old farmer was heartbroken. It was time to break up the hard ground to plant the potatoes – if he didn't do it soon the year would be lost to the crop. He wrote a letter to his son and expressed anguish that hard times were at hand. His son wrote back: "Dad, don't dig up the potato field...that is the place where we stashed the loot!" Within hours, a team of policemen were digging the entire field searching for the proceeds of the theft. Finding nothing, they went home. The next day, the young man wrote from his cell: "Dad, that was the best I could provide to get the ground broke up, and as I have said all along, I didn't steal anything. I hope they got the place ready for you."

The young man cared for his father's need in a way that no one expected – but he was working a plan. That was the same story we read in the Gospels. There was a man accused as a criminal, beaten and executed...but that wasn't the story. The truth was that God provided something they didn't understand in a way that they didn't expect. That is the kind of God we serve.

Though some ignore the Savior's true message in favor of a self-directed life, those who trust Jesus find Him to be the answer God promised long before His coming.

- Jesus is the answer. He created me, and He insists that I yield to Him – and He is right.
- Jesus is the answer when those closest to me are hurting, and I take their need to Him.
- Jesus is the answer when people want to use Him to fix their problems, but want to deny His right to choose when, where and how He works.

He was the answer when His coming was announced three thousand years ago, and He was the answer when He came two thousand years ago. He is still the answer today.

Jesus will be the answer when believers are assaulted by academics, scoffed at by cynics and beheaded by evil men. He will be the answer when the church is hated, and when it is removed. He will be the answer when Israel is brought under the full weight of human hatred. He will be the answer when He comes in the clouds and they "look on Him Whom they have pierced". He will be the answer when His mouth opens and destroys the best weaponry of the world's military machines. Jesus WAS, IS and IS To COME – as the answer to the human need.

Following His Footsteps:
Lesson Ten: "The Paper Cut Test" (Mark 1:16-2:22)

Did you ever get a simple little "paper cut"? Isn't is *unbelievable* that you can be so careful, eat right, exercise, maybe even go off to the gym and really try to get in shape, and a simple piece of paper can wound you in such a way as to distract you all day long? Not long ago, I was trying to organize some notes for a rather detailed speech I had to give to a group up north. One of the last things I do before I am going to make any kind of presentation is to check to see that I have all the pages in the stack, and that they are in the right order. In the process of checking the pages, the stack began to slip away from me, and as I grabbed the falling papers, one cut into my skin in two places between my first two fingers. It wasn't any big deal, and I barely noticed it until *after* the presentation. A group of us decided we would go out for a bite to eat, and the place we went had a special on their renown "corn of the cob." I wanted to give it a try, and used my normal method of dousing the cob in butter, followed by an unhealthy dose of salt. You know where this is going... the salt found its way into both of my paper cuts and suddenly I felt like my fingers were undergoing surgery. I could barely enjoy the meal...obviously I was experiencing a "first world" problem. At this point, some of you may be recognizing me for the true wimp that I am.

It occurs to me that if rocks can be sculpted and cut through by the long term and constant drip of water, if a fully grown adult man can be dislodged by a swarm of tiny bees, if a vast oak tree can be felled by the work of small termites... paper cuts can do significant damage to even the most strong and efficient office workers. Seriously, sometimes it isn't the BIG ISSUES that tear us down – but the steady wear of small ones. It is clear that method of attack was used against the Savior, and it may be used against you as well – so it is worth exploring as we follow the early part of the ministry of Jesus.

Let's remember first that the Savior came to serve His Father and to develop a ministry to people that was both effective and sustainable. He took care to model for us how to care for people, and how to prioritize the work of God as we represent Him before a lost world. At the same time, the Gospel writer included for us something more – the enemy's attack on Jesus' ministry. He attacked every forward move of that ministry – as is his method. Some of the attacks were profound and pronounced. For those, we have been taught to pray fervently, armor up and stick together, huddled around the Word. They come, and in those dramatic moments people are tuned to pray. Yet other attacks are more like the steady wear of "paper cuts" designed to *annoy* and draw spiritual blood and energy from the work. It is now as it was then…

Key Principle: Ministry is not only tested by the more profound struggles, but energy can be significantly drained by steady harassment of the enemy.

There are a number of **weights** on your walk with God and your service to Him that are common among people who want to be used of God to care for and reach others. Since every believer is to be intentional about ministry, it is important that we identify the points fo attack that are used to cause that strain and look for the pattern to overcome their influence:

First, let's recognize the call to make disciples puts a strain on those who do it (Mark 1:16-20; 2:14-22). We'll call it a "drain".

The beginning of Mark's Gospel offers some snapshots of Jesus choosing the disciples near the Sea of Galilee. Let's look at two of them so that we can identify the kinds of pressures disciple making can place on those who follow Jesus by doing it:

Mark 1:16 As He was going along by the Sea of Galilee, He saw Simon and Andrew, the brother of Simon, casting a net in the sea; for they were fishermen. 17

And Jesus said to them, "Follow Me, and I will make you become fishers of men." 18 Immediately they left their nets and followed Him. 19 Going on a little farther, He saw James the son of Zebedee, and John his brother, who were also in the boat mending the nets. 20 Immediately He called them; and they left their father Zebedee in the boat with the hired servants, and went away to follow Him.

Before you keep reading, notice a few things about the disciples that Jesus chose in this little picture.

- First, Jesus called the men from the work they were already doing (Mark 1:16). The men were busy, not idle. Some were casting their nets to fish as in Mark 1:16, while others were mending the nets from the night's work they just completed (1:19).

- Second, Jesus told them that He had a task that was in some ways not wholly unfamiliar, but required they change from what they were doing and follow His lead (Mark 1:17).

- Third, they immediately obeyed and left what they were accomplishing to simply follow the Master.

This is not the only record of the call of the disciples, for they were called more than once. By this time, Jesus was well known to them. They heard His speaking, and some had even traveled with Him on a journey. It is easy to read this like they were new to Jesus, but they weren't, and we know this by cross-checking the other Gospel accounts. In the end, they chose to do what He said and follow Him – that is obvious in the narrative. What is far less recognized is the reverse – that Jesus' life changed by calling them to His side.

To deliberately make disciples is to sign up to be constantly observed, to become intentional about the slightest things. It is a decision to become conscious that people are watching your work and your responses to the normal stresses of life. Your *diet* becomes their *license*. Your favorite song comes under the morally sensitive scrutiny of the follower – are those words really

"God honoring?" Discipleship has its own drain…it places a tiny discomfort, like a "paper cut" that heightens your sensitivity…but the observation of your life by the disciple isn't the only factor that places a strain on your life. Drop down to Mark 2…

Mark 2:14 As He passed by, He saw Levi the son of Alphaeus sitting in the tax booth, and He said to him, "Follow Me!" And he got up and followed Him. 15 And it happened that He was reclining at the table in his house, and many tax collectors and sinners were dining with Jesus and His disciples; for there were many of them, and they were following Him. 16 When the scribes of the Pharisees saw that He was eating with the sinners and tax collectors, they said to His disciples, "Why is He eating and drinking with tax collectors and sinners?" 17 And hearing this, Jesus said to them, "It is not those who are healthy who need a physician, but those who are sick; I did not come to call the righteous, but sinners." 18 John's disciples and the Pharisees were fasting; and they came and said to Him, "Why do John's disciples and the disciples of the Pharisees fast, but Your disciples do not fast?" 19 And Jesus said to them, "While the bridegroom is with them, the attendants of the bridegroom cannot fast, can they? So long as they have the bridegroom with them, they cannot fast. 20 "But the days will come when the bridegroom is taken away from them, and then they will fast in that day. 21 "No one sews a patch of unshrunk cloth on an old garment; otherwise the patch pulls away from it, the new from the old, and a worse tear results. 22 "No one puts new wine into old wineskins; otherwise the wine will burst the skins, and the wine is lost and the skins as well; but one puts new wine into fresh wineskins."

Here, the passage reveals other stresses that were placed on Jesus as He chose disciples that we should make note of as well.

First, the people chosen by the Master quickly focused scrutiny on Him. Some with religious titles were acutely aware that

Jesus' choices were not what they would have chosen – and that became the subject of criticism. All this, and the disciples hadn't done yet anything but eat dinner! Jesus found Himself answering criticism concerning His choices (Mark 2:17), and acknowledging that the men were not the healthiest lot – but those with great spiritual need. Here is the point: disciples are needy, and they will require something of your life – and that is the reason we would rather offer classes as a church than personally make disciples. All of us are under the pressures of daily life, and we can easily excuse our distance from others as a necessity in our busy world. Yet, discipleship – deliberate patterning and encouragement is our call – and we know it. We keep hoping that classes will do the trick, even when it seems obvious that we offer so little time compared to the number of hours the world offers to press young believers into its mold.

A second factor involved in the criticism was not simply the choice of disciples, but the methodology and practices taught to the learners (Mark 2:18-19). Jesus chose the men and not everyone like who He chose – but they also "weighed in" on what He trained them to practice. "Why not fasting like John's disciples?" they asked. Discipleship raised the scrutiny of other "experts" and Jesus didn't get a passing grade in their evaluation. The truth is that discipleship and training draws the trainer under the scrutiny of those who are not even engaged in the process. Everyone has an opinion about how to do it, even if they aren't doing it.

The objective of making disciples is one that will put a strain on your life. When people are watching, you must be even more careful. When people are learning, you must be intentional. When people are following, you must act as a leader. It isn't a bad thing, but it isn't an easy thing either. **Ask a parent**!

Imagine you take your child into a market to pick up a few things, and they are not feeling well. Teeth are causing pain and a slight fever. The otherwise pleasant child is fussy and uncomfortable. You know what is wrong, and you are letting them fuss a bit to get things selected and get home where you can administer a little gum soother and get them to sleep. It will all be fine in a few minutes. As you pass people and they look in the cart at your little bundle of fussiness, each offers advice. "If you just pick him up and rock him, he'll settle right down!" the woman behind you says. "Thanks!" you mutter, as if you hadn't thought of that. Everyone feels the right to give instructions, but they aren't going home with you, and don't know the whole picture of what you are doing with the child. Discipleship draws criticism... and it often comes from people who are not engaged in the process a whit. Criticism can sting like a little enduring paper cut.

I am not complaining about the call to make disciples – it is a fantastic and rewarding part of our call! I am, however, making the observation that with obedience to that call you will add strain to your life. Everything valuable in life comes at a price, and obedience in making disciples is no different. We cannot engage the process without recognizing the drain it will put on us, or we miss part of the lesson of the verses God included to instruct us.

Second, the enemy offers resistance to any forward movement that will cost him (Mark 1:21-28). We'll call this "disruption".

Beyond the strain of criticism and inspection is another very important truth that we need to reckon with – there is an enemy at work to defeat us. Go back to Mark 1...

Mark 1:21 They went into Capernaum; and immediately on the Sabbath He entered the synagogue and began to teach. 22 They were amazed at His teaching; for He was teaching them as one having authority, and not as the scribes. 23 Just then there was a man in their synagogue with an unclean spirit; and he cried out, 24 saying, "What business do we have with each other, Jesus of Nazareth? Have You come to destroy us? I know who You are-the Holy One of God!" 25 And Jesus rebuked him, saying, "Be quiet, and come out of him!" 26 Throwing him into convulsions, the unclean spirit cried out with a loud voice and came out of him. 27 They were all amazed, so that they debated among themselves, saying, "What is this? A new teaching with authority! He commands even the unclean spirits, and they obey Him." 28 Immediately the news about Him spread everywhere into all the surrounding district of Galilee.

We usually anticipate the opposition when it concerns evangelism, but that isn't the only place planned snares of the enemy will trip us. When we help disciples move out of bondage and into a fuller walk with God, the enemy is still losing ground - and that will come with stiff resistance – because he doesn't like losing ground! In fact, a deceived and ensnared believer is often a more powerful a weapon in the hand of the enemy as one who is still spiritually dead. Go back to the story…

Jesus took the disciples to the synagogue because it was Sabbath, and He taught the crowd that gathered in Capernaum to listen. He spoke directly, and made clear sense. As the people began to respond to TRUTH, the voice of the enemy DISTRACTED people from the "life-filled words" of the Master. There are a number of truths that are important in this passage:

Note first that the enemy was lurking in the synagogue… because the enemy does some of his best work in religious places.

Second, note that nothing they said was UNTRUE, it was simply distracting Jesus from the forward progress of teaching. The demonic presence simply raised questions and made distractions that pulled the class off track. Have you ever seen something like this? I don't mean that you sat next to someone who murmured like they were possessed… I mean someone who drew the class off track, week after week, only to confound, confuse and disrupt. They didn't learn, and they didn't let others learn. The veteran teachers know what I am referring to in this… the enemy works both in deception and in distraction – and we must recognize the difference between real questions and disruptions.

Recently I engaged a young man who asked many questions about God, about belief and generally about my faith. His questions were complex, and they took time to answer in detail to be sure that I was saying things that were both Biblical and clear. I spent a number of hours on each question. Weeks wore on, he wrote question after question and I answered diligently. I prayed over each answer and asked God to make clear how I should proceed. I felt a real strain on the load this added to the week, but I didn't want to drop the ball on a sacred trust – God may have brought this man into my life to draw him to God – and I didn't want to be slack on my responsibility in this area. After a few more questions, I made the point that I had done my best with every question, so I wanted to ask him a question of my own… "Was he serious in the questions he raised?" I asked. He replied, and I admit I was floored by his response. "Not at all!" he said. "I just wanted to tie up your time and keep you from teaching other people about your God fantasies." I was shocked, but I was thankful that God answered my prayer, and I learned a lesson. Everything you and I are offered is either an opportunity or a distraction – and it will take maturity to know the difference.

Jesus took control of the message, and cast out the demon – causing others to recognize His power. God's Word isn't open to sharing the stage with anyone else's word – and Jesus took care of the problem. Yet, it came at a cost. We look at FAME as a GOOD thing, but that is not always the case. Some of the most effective ministries I know of are not well known around the world – but they are incredibly effective. In our modern "Madison Avenue" view of ministry, we cannot easily understand why Jesus may not have wanted to be too well known at this point in the ministry – but the enemy knew that POPULARITY can swamp the boat – and that can become the most effective way to pull a ministry down.

Distraction is something that can happen to any work of God – large or small. Believers need to be able to measure God at work by many standards – not simply "popularity" or parking lot sizes. When we use modern business metrics to measure ministry effectiveness, we lose sight that God works in different ways in different places. The measure of a ministry should be how well it accomplishes sustainable work within its consistent and Biblically infused vision.

The point is that Jesus didn't need to be that well known yet, and the enemy couldn't wait to make Him the hottest thing on the block. What looked like a great acknowledgement of Jesus' power was actually a pressure hold applied by the enemy who wanted to get Jesus' popularity rating boosted to the point of ministry hindrance. Even viral popularity can become a problem to sustainable ministry. It can become a "paper cut" that hinders growing people because the program takes over… and it is something mature believers need to be careful about.

It is true that discipleship is a call of God that puts a drain on your life. It is easier to navigate life without pulling along someone else. It is also true that we face an enemy who wants to find ways to distract us from focusing on the growth and development of people – in favor of other notions of popularity and success that fill our hearts but are not from our Father above. Yet, there are other "paper cuts" that can distract us…

Third, we should consider that a drain of physical limitations can distract progress (Mark 1:29-31). We'll call this "distraction".

Jesus and the boys were just beginning to get the work in Capernaum going, and one of the people who provided meals and care for the men was taken ill…

*Mark 1:29 And immediately after they came out of the synagogue, they came into the house of Simon and Andrew, with James and John. 30 Now **Simon's mother-in-law was lying sick with a fever**; and immediately they spoke to Jesus about her. 31 And He came to her and **raised her up**, taking her by the hand, and the fever left her, and **she waited on them**.*

What is clear is the fact that Peter's mother in law was an asset to the ministry, as she took care of the men again as soon as she was well. Her "down time" slowed the ministry, because a servant was knocked off her feet. Don't miss that detail…

I am not being "spooky" when I admit the enemy can get permission from our Father to attack the ministry and add extra "drag" by attacking our health. He can attack our feelings, our digestion, our sleepiness – an array of symptomatic attacks. He did it in a pronounced way with Job in the Bible, but that isn't the only time he did it. In Mark 1 he wanted to slow down the work at home and keep the men busy and strained to do the little "normal" things of life, he wanted to Simon to worry about his mother-in-law and be distracted from the growing ministry. Don't miss that Satan was at work on both public popularity and private distraction – that is one of the combinations that often lands in the life of God's servant. While the pressure mounted in the public eye for Jesus to do more and more, private pressures at home made the rising popularity seem even harder to navigate – and that was the point of the two-pronged attack. Jesus healed the women, but while He did, He surely recognized the play the enemy was making.

Fourth, even misdirected followers can easily disrupt ministry and help the enemy (Mark 1:32-32, 39-45). We'll call this what it is: "disobedience".

One of the common attacks of the enemy that I have profoundly noticed over the years is the aid they inadvertently offer the deceiver by being **blatantly disobedient to the Word of God** – all the while thinking they are aiding God's cause. Let's look at the case offered in Mark 1…

*Mark 1:32 When evening came, after the sun had set, they began bringing to Him all who were ill and those who were demon-possessed. 33 And the whole city had gathered at the door. 34 And He healed many who were ill with various diseases, and cast out many demons; and He was not permitting the demons to speak, because they knew who He was… 39 And He went into their synagogues throughout all Galilee, preaching and casting out the demons. 40 And a **leper** came to Jesus, beseeching Him and falling on his knees before Him, and saying, "If You are willing, **You can make me*** *clean." 41 Moved with compassion, Jesus stretched out His hand and touched him, and said to him, "I am willing; be cleansed." 42 Immediately the leprosy left him and he was cleansed. 43 And He sternly warned him and immediately sent him away, 44 and He said to him, "See that you say nothing to anyone; but go, show yourself to the priest and offer for your cleansing what Moses commanded, as a testimony to them." 45 But he went out and began to proclaim it freely and to spread the news around, to such an extent that Jesus could no longer publicly enter a city, but stayed out in unpopulated areas; and they were coming to Him from everywhere.*

The enemy was already at work trying to get the public ministry of Jesus to rise in popularity so fast that He would be **unable to focus on the development of the men**, and be **inundated with public fame**. Demons didn't want clear teaching, so they disrupted at the synagogue. Now they used a needy man that came to Jesus, but then didn't follow His words obediently… the man had a plan to "help God" without the need to be weighed down by obedience to God. He came needing healing, as we all do. He came ready to receive from Jesus.

Note verse 42, Jesus completely healed him and he was clean. Now look at the words of the next verse very carefully. In all of the Gospels, have you read of any time when Jesus spoke and "sternly warned" anyone? It seems the demeanor of the Savior was serious and sober as he looked at the now healed man. "Say NOTHING to ANYONE except the priest." Those were Jesus' words. They sound straight and to the point. They were neither complicated, nor confusing. Yet, the man disobeyed in short order, all the while thinking he was doing something GOOD for God.

We need to rehearse, again and again in our lives, **there is no substitute for obedience** to God's commands. We do not know what God knows, nor do we see what He sees. Our stubborn need to control must not be allowed to drive us from our knees and back onto the throne of our life while under the delusion we are helping God. We are NOT. The tragic end of King Saul came from that very decision – to do what he thought would help God MORE than to accept the instruction from God and follow it precisely.

The man was disobedient to the word of Jesus, and it caused a mess for Jesus. How often I have observed this attack of the enemy, facilitated by a believer who blissfully thinks careful knowledge of and obedience to the Word is less important than the "clear fame" they brought to Jesus. Reach a nation in disobedience and you have accomplished a great victory for the enemy – because God desires obedience more than anything else... period. Believers carving their own path cause constant and irritating "paper cut" wounds on believers and ministry workers who are trying to follow the Word – it is both distracting and hurtful.

Fifth, there is a constant weight placed by those who misunderstand God's method of direction that can confuse ministry workers (Mark 1:35-38). We'll call this "delusion."

Jesus got alone, but the disciples didn't understand the essential nature of His time with the Father – because many people think ministry is a physical pursuit – with a little "nod" to the spiritual realm. They don't get how the world really works, let alone how ministry works...

*Mark 1:35 In the early morning, while it was still dark, Jesus got up, left the house, and went away to a **secluded** place, and was **praying** there. 36 Simon and his **companions searched for Him;** 37 they found Him, and said to Him, "Everyone is looking for You." 38 **He said** to them, **"Let us go somewhere else** to the towns nearby, so that I may preach there also; for that is what I came for."*

The disciples pressed for more and more ministry without breaking away and recognizing the need to seek the Father in Heaven. Jesus got alone because He needed to commune and exemplify the need to seek the direction from above. The disciples were living the "rat race of ministry" while Jesus was getting alone. His alone time re-energized the Lord.

People caught in a "rat race" – even of ministry events – cannot lead like Jesus. There is a difference between being full in your schedule and being driven by it. Jesus understood the need for solitude and searching out the Father's heart for ministry before taking on the next task. The men were ready for the "next big thing" while Jesus was communing with His Father, and getting re-energized.

Jesus knew how to get alone with His Father. It is worth noting that the devil miscalculated the strength of that alone time at the temptation. Jesus was physically hungry, but His time away left Him spiritually full. His denial of the physical helped Him to stay focused on His walk before the Father and not get sidetracked by lesser things. His responses to the devil showed that Jesus valued the study of the Scriptures in the "good times" - for Jesus knew the Word and was able to recall it when needed.

This is a common mistake: people see ministry as primarily a physical pursuit, and measure its growth in buildings, budgets and bodies in the pew – but those metrics don't tell the story. Eleven disciples transformed in heart would eventually yield much more than five thousand spectators deeply moved at their full bellies. The DELUSION is a common one, and it creeps into ministry all the time: the focus on the physical as the point of ministry. Look at the little story in Mark 2…

Mark 2:1 When He had come back to Capernaum several days afterward, it was heard that He was at home. 2 And many were gathered together, so that there was no longer room, not even near the door; and He was speaking the word to them. 3 And they came, bringing to Him a paralytic, carried by four men. 4 Being unable to get to Him because of the crowd, they removed the roof above Him; and when they had dug an opening, they let down the pallet on which the paralytic was lying. 5 And Jesus seeing their faith said to the paralytic, "Son, your sins are forgiven." 6 But some of the scribes were sitting there and reasoning in their hearts, 7 "Why does this man speak that way? He is blaspheming; who can forgive sins but God alone?" 8 Immediately Jesus, aware in His spirit that they were reasoning that way within themselves, said to them, "Why are you reasoning about these things in your hearts? 9 "Which is easier, to say to the paralytic, 'Your sins are forgiven '; or to say, 'Get up, and pick up your pallet and walk '? 10 "But so that you may know that the Son of Man has authority on earth to forgive sins "-He said to the paralytic, 11 "I say to you, get up, pick up your pallet and go home." 12 And he got up and immediately picked up the pallet and went out in the sight of everyone, so that they were all amazed and were glorifying God, saying, "We have never seen anything like this." 13 And He went out again by the seashore; and all the people were coming to Him, and He was teaching them.

Jesus healed the man's heart, and the work was essentially DONE. His sin forgiven, Jesus did the part that only He can do. That didn't satisfy the scribes. They thought it was a hoax, because they measured ministry by externals – by physical markers. The man needed life inside, not simply working legs.

There is an old story I have used before, but it illustrates well the problem of looking at externals when the internals are the real issue:

I heard about a man who saw his dog walking across his lawn with his neighbors dead cat in his mouth. The man was horrified to see that the dog had apparently killed the neighbor's beloved cat. He was determined to hide this embarrassing and heart-wrenching situation from the neighbor. He took the cat from the dog's mouth and proceeded to wash the animal gingerly, to brush the fur and make the animal look well kept. That night he slipped over to the neighbor's porch and placed the cat quietly beside the door. He left undetected. The next morning before work his neighbor was in the driveway visibly shaken. "What's wrong?" he asked, feigning concern. The neighbor replied, "It is the strangest thing I ever seen. Fluffy got hit by a car yesterday. We had a funeral service for her in the backyard. But, when we got up this morning we found the hole empty and the body of our now clean cat clean on the back porch." (adapted from sermon central illustrations).

Here is the problem: The man tried to clean the cat outwardly, but he couldn't change the fact that the cat was dead. A lot of people think that is what ministry is really all about. They try to change the outward appearance, or deal with the outward need. They feed the hungry, house the homeless and try to act kindly – and that is good – but it isn't the primary need. It is part of the DELUSION that spiritual things can be seen clearly through the physical eye. When ministry is measured that way, it discourages and weighs down those who are working in the spiritual realm.

- Discipleship is wonderful, but it drains your energy.
- Forward moving ministry is exciting, but it draws the attention of an enemy that disrupts.
- Servanthood is essential, but the needs of the body can be a distraction.
- Jesus is delivering men, but disobedience unsettles the ministry.
- Ministry needs press God's workers, but we must be directed and measured by spiritual metrics.

I recall years ago in Elkhart, Indiana, finding out that a neighbor was tapping off my friend's electricity, and she was being charged for power usage that she didn't ever get. She went away on vacation during the heat of the summer, and turned off most all of her electrical appliances. When she came home, she noticed the meter spinning wildly on the pole, and couldn't figure out what where the power was going. We traced the lines, and found the neighbor was using a line strung from her house to theirs. Knowing where your power is going is important. God is at work through many, and some of them are tired, but haven't figured out where their energy is being tapped. The model of Jesus can help us spot some of the ways power is pulled from its rightful place.

Other volumes in the series through the Bible are available through amazon.com and can be found by searching for:

"Dr. Randall D. Smith"

Free teaching resources are also available at:

www.randalldsmith.com

www.ingramcontent.com/pod-product-compliance
Lightning Source LLC
Chambersburg PA
CBHW060510030426
42337CB00015B/1830